Rethinking America

Rethinking America

Advanced Readings in U.S. Culture

M. E. SOKOLIK

Heinle & Heinle Publishers
A Division of Wadsworth, Inc.
Boston, Massachusetts 02116 U.S.A.

Vice President and Publisher: Stanley J. Galek
Editorial Director: David C. Lee
Assistant Editor: Kenneth Mattsson
Project Manager: Stacey Sawyer, Sawyer & Williams
Production Supervisor: Patricia Jalbert
Manufacturing Coordinator: Lisa McLaughlin
Text Design: Nancy Benedict
Front Matter Design: Adriane Bosworth
Photo Research: Judy Mason
Illustrations: Anne Eldridge, HieroGraphics
Cover Design: Amy Wasserman

Manufactured in the United States of America.

Heinle & Heinle Publishers is a division of Wadsworth, Inc.

Library of Congress Cataloging-in-Publication Data

Sokolik, M. E. (Margaret E.)
    Rethinking America : advanced readings in U.S. culture / M.E. Sokolik.
      p. cm.
    Includes index.
    ISBN 0-8384-2277-2
    1. Readers—United States. 2. English language—Textbooks for foreign
speakers. 3. United States—Civilization—Problems, exercises, etc.
I. Title.
PE1127.H5S67 1992
428.6'4—dc20
                                         91-43313
                                           CIP

10 9 8 7 6 5 4 3 2

**For my mother
Velma Fitzsimmons**

Contents

3   THE BARE NECESSITIES   49

4   FRIENDS AND RELATIONS   71

5   THE AMERICAN LANDSCAPE   95

Preface

Rethinking America arises out of a need felt in many ESL classrooms, my own included, for readings and information that allow the international student entry into the dialogue of U.S. culture.

This text integrates different types of readings—essays, short stories, speeches, news stories—with questions for discussion, vocabulary development, writing, and various related activities that can be either teacher- or student-directed. *Rethinking America* encourages cultural comparison, allows the students the opportunity to examine their own cultural values, and integrates activities that ask the student to learn more on their own from their interactions with native English-speaking Americans.

All these exercises and activities are aimed at promoting not only improvement of English language skills, but enhancement of cultural understanding through lively and relevant readings.

ORGANIZATION

Chapter Organization

Each chapter is organized around a central theme and divided into two subthemes. Each subtheme contains two readings that examine the topic from different points of view.

Introductory Materials

Before You Read

Each reading is introduced by graphic or tabular information relating to the topic. A brief summary of the reading follows that information, and then the student is asked to think about one or two questions before reading the passage.

Glossary

For some readings, there may be vocabulary that is difficult to find in traditional college dictionaries or that refers to people or places that the student may be unfamiliar with. In these cases, a glossary is included before the reading that defines or explains these unfamiliar terms.

About the Author

Brief biographies of most authors are included for the student's information.

The Reading

Each reading includes line numbers for easy reference by the student and teacher.

End Materials

Check Your Comprehension

Following each reading are three or more questions regarding the factual content of the reading.

Vocabulary

Also following each reading is a vocabulary exercise. These exercises vary from reading to reading.

Think About It

In this section, questions ask students to go beyond the factual content of the reading and relate their own knowledge of and experience with the theme of the article or story. The final question in this section involves a project that encourages classroom group work or work outside class conducting surveys, watching television programs, and so forth.

Synthesis

At the end of each chapter, a section of exercises and activities helps the student integrate the various ideas presented in the four readings in the chapter.

Discussion and Debate

This section presents several questions that could be used for class discussion or debate. The final question in this section is the same in all chapters: it asks the student to think of an additional question about the chapter to ask his/her classmates.

Writing Topics

The writing topics present different levels of writing, from simple question-answer or single-paragraph writing, to letters and complete essays.

On Your Own

This section gives several ideas for independent study and development of the topics of the chapter. The activities are entirely student-centered.

ACKNOWLEDGMENTS

It would be impossible to acknowledge all of the people who have contributed in some way to the development of this text. First, and foremost, I would like to thank my students at Harvard and MIT, who patiently and with good humor were the testing ground for much of the material found herein. I would also like to thank the ESL program at Harvard University, particularly its director, Ann Dow, for allowing me to pilot the idea by approving my proposal for a course in American popular culture.

I would like to thank some of my colleagues, past and present—Sharon Hilles, California State Polytechnic University at Pomona, for getting me into this business in the first place, and Peter Master, California State University at Fresno, for his enthusiasm and treasured friendship. I also thank Suzanne Flynn, MIT, Donna Lardiere, Boston University, Christopher Sawyer-Lauçanno, MIT, and John Schumann, UCLA.

My editor, David Lee, also deserves my thanks for his optimism, support, and fine suggestions which helped shape this manuscript. I would also like to thank the following reviewers whose critical comments were an important part in the development of this book. Their names are:

Ardis Flenniken (California State University)

Joanne Harris (Illinois Benedictine College)

Brian Hickey (Manhattanville College)

Bjarne Nielsen (Central Piedmont Community College)

Carole Rosen (Hunter College)

As always I would like to thank my husband, Michael Smith, for his gentle nagging, encouragement, and support while this text was being prepared.

1
Economics

PART ONE
Money: The Almighty Dollar

Before You Read

Table 1.1   Median Family Income
(in today's dollars)

1960	$ 5,620
1970	8,734
1975	11,800
1980	17,710
1985	23,618
1987	25,986

Source: Bureau of the Census,
*Statistical Abstract of the United
States, 1989* (Washington, D.C., 1989),
table 712.

The United States' economic system, based on the principles of
capitalism, is often said to produce materialistic values in the country's
citizens, who care too much about money and possessions. In the following reading, the authors discuss briefly the basis of this materialism
and of other American cultural values.

Before you read, think about these questions:

- Are Americans too concerned with wealth?

- What kinds of attitudes about wealth do people in your own culture have?

About the Authors

Conrad M. Arensberg and Arthur N. Niehoff are American anthropolo-
gists and editors of the book *Introducing Social Change*, from which
this excerpt was taken.

American Cultural Values

by Conrad M. Arensberg and Arthur N. Niehoff

The rich resources of America, along with the extraordinary growth of its industrial economy, have brought a widespread wealth of material goods such as the world has not seen before. There has been a wholesale development and diffusion of the marvels of modern comfort—
5 swift and pleasant transportation, central heating, air conditioning, instant hot and cold water, electricity, and laborsaving devices of endless variety. The high value placed on such comforts has caused industries to be geared to produce ever greater quantities and improved versions. Americans seem to feel that they have a "right" to such amenities.

10 Achievement and success are measured primarily by the quantity of material goods one possesses, both because these are abundant and because they indicate how much money an individual earns. This material evidence of personal worth is modified by the credit system; but still, credit purchases will carry an individual only so far, after which credit
15 agencies will refuse to advance more without evidence of fundamental wealth.

Since there is little display value in the size of one's paycheck or bank account, the average individual buys prestige articles that others can see: expensive clothing or furniture, a fine car, a swimming pool, an
20 expensive home, or one of the endless variety of devices that may have other functions but can also readily be seen by visitors—power mowers, barbeque paraphernalia, television, and stereophonic systems. A person's status is affected to a secondary degree by his level of education, type of occupation, and social behavior; but even these qualities seem
25 to be significant only in terms of how much income they help him to obtain. Thus, a college professor who has earned his Ph.D. will have less status in the general community than a business executive or film actor who has no college education but commands a much larger salary.

Excerpted from Conrad M. Arensberg and Arthur N. Niehoff, eds., *Introducing Social Change* (Chicago: Aldine-Atherton, Inc., 1971).

Check Your Comprehension

1. According to the authors, how is status achieved in American culture?

2. How important is education to a person's status?

3. How is status most likely to be exhibited by an average American?

Vocabulary: In Context

1. *Wholesale* (line 3) is closest in meaning to:
   a. cheap, inexpensive
   b. large, unlimited
   c. not retail

2. *Amenities* (line 9) is closest in meaning to:
   a. things that improve one's life
   b. friendships
   c. religious beliefs

3. If something has *little display value* (line 17), it:
   a. has a low price
   b. cannot be shown to other people
   c. is too small to read

4. *Paraphernalia* (line 22) is closest in meaning to:
   a. fire
   b. food
   c. equipment

5. *Commands* (line 28) is closest in meaning to:
   a. directs
   b. deserves
   c. controls

Think About It

1. What are some of the "side effects" of modern comforts?

2. Why do you think a movie actor has more "status" than a college professor? Do you think this value is appropriate?

3. How are attitudes about wealth in your own culture different from or similar to American ones?

4. (i) Which of the following things do *you* think are prestigious? Place a check mark on the line next to each one.
   (ii) Now ask an "average American" which items he or she finds prestigious. Place a check mark on each of those lines.

	YOU	"AVERAGE AMERICAN"
a. Having a Ph.D. in English	_____	_____
b. Having a Ph.D. in economics	_____	_____
c. Owning a bank	_____	_____
d. Owning a flower shop	_____	_____
e. Hiring a full-time babysitter ($15,000 per year)	_____	_____
f. Hiring a full-time housekeeper ($15,000 per year)	_____	_____
g. Eating in a French restaurant ($50.00)	_____	_____
h. Eating in an American restaurant ($50.00)	_____	_____
i. Owning an American pickup truck ($25,000)	_____	_____
j. Owning a German sedan ($25,000)	_____	_____

(iii) How are your choices different from the average American's?

(iv) Finally, looking at pairs a–b, c–d, etc., would one item of each pair be considered more prestigious than the other? Since money is not the most important factor in these choices, what other factors could influence "prestige"?

Before You Read

Table 1.2   Consumer Credit 1987

number of credit card owners	107,200,000
number of credit cards	841,000,000
dollars spent using credit cards	$374,800,000,000
total credit card debt	$152,500,000,000

Source: *The Nilson Report*, HSN Consultants (Los Angeles, 1988).

As table 1.2 shows, many Americans depend on credit to purchase the things they want. A recent trend in credit has been "gold" credit cards, which offer the user more services and, some might say, more "prestige."

The following article tells of one man's experience with a "prestige" credit card.

Before you read, think about these questions:

- How are most purchases made in your culture (for example, with cash, checks, credit cards, or some other system)?
- Do you have any credit cards? If not, would you like to?

Glossary

Fort Lauderdale   City in the state of Florida; the headquarters of the American Express Corporation are found there.

Toys "Я" Us   Large chain of toy stores

About the Author

Bob Greene is a journalist who writes for many newspapers and magazines. He has written several books as well.

Platinum Card

by Bob Greene

He had an embarrassed, furtive sound to his voice. He said he had a confession to make.

"I got the American Express Platinum Card," he said. He was referring to the new credit cards that are sold for $250 a year to the top eche-
5 lon of American Express's charge-card customers.

"You really have one?" I said.

"You can't use my name," he hurriedly said. "I'm a funeral director, and it wouldn't look good for the families around here to think that I'm spending their hard-earned money on something like the Platinum Card."

10 I asked him to tell me the whole story. "Start at the beginning," I said.

"Well, first I just had the regular American Express green card," he said. "I thought that was a pretty good card to have. Then we were at lunch at Kon-Tiki Ports, and the bill came. I gave the waiter my card. He
15 came back and said, 'I'm sorry, but it's going to be a while. There's a problem with the phone lines, and we have to wait to get verification on your card.'

"My friend who was with me whipped out his Gold Card. He said, 'Will we have to wait with this?' The waiter said, 'No *sir!* Right away!'
20 "They said *sir* to him. They never said *sir* to me. I thought, 'Phooey on this. I need a Gold Card!'"

So he applied for one and he got it. American Express's regular green cards cost $35 a year; the Gold Cards cost $65 a year. But he figured it was worth it.

25 Then, earlier this year, he looked at an American Express imprinting machine in a restaurant. There were decals on it showing the regular green card and Gold Card. But there was a new decal, too: the Platinum Card.

"I asked the person at the restaurant about it," he said. "He told me
30 that the Platinum Card costs $250 a year, and only the very elite of American Express's customers could get one.

"I had to do it. I called American Express and asked how I could get a Platinum Card. The person on the phone was very snotty about it. The person said, '*We* will determine who receives a Platinum Card. You can-
35 not *apply* for it. You must be *invited*.' Very aloof.

"Part of me realized that there is something very warped about a society that tells you that you can pay $250 for a charge card that has a different color to it than your regular charge card—and you actually want the $250 card anyway.

40   "But each day I looked in my mail for an invitation. It didn't come and it didn't come. I felt brokenhearted. I wasn't good enough for the Platinum Card. I wondered what I had done to get American Express mad at me.

    "Each day I woke up and thought, 'Maybe this is the day.' Each day
45 passed, and I wasn't one of the chosen people.

    "But then it happened. In October, it came. The envelope was like parchment. There were platinum lines all over it. It made me feel like someone was asking me to marry their daughter.

    "I opened it up. It was an invitation to obtain a Platinum Card. Not
50 an application—an invitation.

    "I sent my check for $250 in. When the card came, it was in an envelope from Fort Lauderdale. This is no kidding—I took it in the bathroom to open it up. I didn't want anyone else around.

    "Inside me, a little voice was saying 'You're living a double stan-
55 dard.' I told the little voice to shut up.

    "I had to use it right away. So I went down to a Toys "Я" Us store to buy a video game cartridge for one of my kids. Very casually, I handed my new Platinum Card to the girl behind the counter.

    "All she said is, 'I'm new here, I've never done an American Express
60 card before. I have to get the manager.' The manager came up and he just processed the card. No big reaction. No bells ringing. People were standing behind me in line—no reaction from them either. I felt like I wanted to cry. I had just laid a Platinum Card on them—and nothing.

    "I went home and walked in the house with a big smile on my face.
65 I said to my wife, 'Guess what I got?' I whipped out my Platinum Card. She said, 'That's nice, dear.' I said, 'No, honey, you don't understand. This is a *Platinum Card.* She said, 'Yes, honey. An American Express Card.'"

He said it was all downhill from there. So far, there has been virtually no reaction to the Platinum Card he spent $250 for. Once he took
70 a friend to lunch, and when he paid for it with his Platinum Card, he thought he noticed two men at the next table looking over and smiling.

    "But after lunch I kept asking myself: Were they smiling or were they smirking? Did they think I was one of life's special few for having a Platinum Card? Or did they think I was a jerk for putting out $250 for a
75 credit card?"

In his dark moments, he has had a troubling thought: "I see them sitting around in the American Express boardroom, and suddenly one of the big corporate bosses says: 'I need a new pool in my back yard. Let's color some of our cards platinum and see if we get some suckers
80 to pay $250 for them.'"

He said that every time he pulls out his Platinum Card now, he's not sure how he should feel. "It doesn't exactly give you a warm feeling, like sex or a hot toddy," he said. "But there's a definite twinge you feel in your ego."

85   So what was the final answer, I asked. Did his Platinum Card make him feel like a special person or like a sucker?

"I feel like a special type of sucker," he said.

From Bob Greene, *Cheeseburgers* (New York: Ballantine Books, 1985).

Check Your Comprehension

1. What is the difference between an American Express Green Card, Gold Card, and Platinum Card?

2. Why do you think the waiter responded differently to the Gold Card?

3. Why was the funeral director embarrassed about his Platinum Card?

Vocabulary: Slang and Colloquial Language

Complete the sentences below with a colloquial word or phrase chosen from the following group.

pretty good   whip out   phooey   shut up
downhill   sucker   snotty   jerk

1. I felt like a _____ when I told my friend to _____ .

2. "_____ on this," John said. "I'm not standing in the rain

    to buy tickets. I'm no _____ ."

3. That movie won't win any Academy Awards, but it was _____ .

    It went _____ after the chase scene.

4. Before I could _____ my money, Mary paid for lunch.

5. "You have a bad attitude," Bill said. "Don't be so _____ ."

Think About It

1. If you were invited, would you accept the Platinum Card? Why or why not?

2. Do you think there are advantages to having credit cards? If so, what are they? If not, why not?

3. Look through a magazine or newspaper for an advertisement for a credit card. What kinds of services does it provide? How does the ad try to appeal to the reader?

4. Imagine you work for a credit-card company. Invent a *new* credit card that will be more prestigious than the platinum card.

Color or name of card: _____

Cost per year: _____

By application or invitation? _____

If by application, what requirements will you have?

_____

_____

_____

If by invitation, what sort of person will you invite?

_____

_____

_____

Often, credit-card companies offer additional services—for example, insurance for car rentals and gifts for spending certain amounts of money per year. Besides credit, what additional services will your new improved card offer?

_____

_____

_____

_____

_____

_____

PART TWO
Housing: A Roof over One's Head

Before You Read

Table 1.3 New Houses Built in the United States

Year	Number	Year	Number
1900	189,000	1970	1,469,000
1925	937,000	1980	1,313,000
1950	1,952,000	1985	1,745,000
1960	1,296,000		

Sources: Department of Commerce, *Housing Construction Statistics, 1900–1965*, and *Construction Reports, Housing Starts, 1970–83*.

This reading addresses the issue of home ownership in the United States. It comes from a book that explains the process of home buying for consumers who may be considering buying their first home.

Before you read, think about the following questions:

- Do you think home ownership is important? Why or why not?
- Do you know what percentage of people in your country own their own homes?

Glossary

Energy Belt Southern states, especially Texas and Louisiana, involved in the production of oil and natural gas

About the Author

Bob Vila is a popular television figure who once hosted a television series *This Old House* on public television. He is also the author of books on building and restoring houses.

Do You Really Want to Buy a House?

by Bob Vila

Home ownership is the heart of what we call the American Dream. It stands for many of the things we value about our way of life. It's one way we think about progress, and for a lot of us, it's one of the definitions of success.

5   And from the depths of the Great Depression of the 1930s right on up to 1980, the progress in this respect was steady. In 1935, home ownership was confined to less than 30 percent of the population. By 1980, very nearly two thirds of the American people (65.8 percent, to be exact) lived in their own home.

10   But then the steady growth stopped and started falling back. By 1987 the home-ownership rate had declined to 63.4 percent, 2.4 points below the 1980 high.

Why did this happen? The basic reason for the turnaround is simply that home ownership, which was never cheap to begin with, has gotten

15   more and more expensive.

The following facts will bear this out, and I suggest that all prospective buyers think about them carefully.

Ownership costs are increasing more rapidly than income. In 1970, the median family income in the United States was $9,700 a year,

20   and the median price of a single-family dwelling was about $23,000.

By 1987, though the median family income had risen by almost 100 percent, to $18,934, the median housing price had risen by 366 percent, to $83,400. In some areas of the country the rate of increase has been even greater.

25   *Steadily larger cash down payments are being demanded.* Ten years ago the standard (20 percent) down payment on an average house required about a third of the average annual family income. Today the down payment represents more than half of what the average family earns in a year. In the nation's highest-priced markets along the West

30   and East coasts, that ratio can approach 75 percent.

Monthly Principal and Interest (P&I) payments have soared. In 1970 the monthly mortgage payment on the median-priced ($23,000) house, with 20 percent down, a thirty-year term, and an interest rate of 8.5 percent, would have been $141.49. If you had bought the median-

35   priced house in 1987, again putting up 20 percent as a down payment, your monthly principal and interest payments for a thirty-year mortgage at 10 percent would have been $591.70. That's an increase of 318 percent!

The impact of these rising costs falls most heavily on younger
40 *buyers.* In 1980, almost two thirds of Americans between the ages of
twenty-five and thirty-four owned their own homes. That set a historical record. But by the end of 1987 this proportion had fallen from two
thirds to little more than one half.

Mortgage foreclosures are increasing. The number of home-
45 mortgage foreclosures has soared in recent years in some areas of the
country, notably in the economically depressed Energy Belt. You read
every day about people in Texas and Louisiana and some areas of the
Midwest walking away from homes they can no longer afford, homes
that are now worth less than the amount outstanding on the mortgage.
50 That prospect has to be a bit unnerving to anyone thinking about buying a home.

But don't let me discourage you! If I'm not selling real estate, I'm
not warning against it, either. I'm simply saying that it's harder to buy a
home than it used to be, not that it's impossible. If you're a first-time
55 buyer today, you'll have to look harder, be more creative, and display a
greater willingness to compromise than you would have had to twenty
or so years ago. The house of your dreams may be beyond your reach,
but the dream of home ownership doesn't have to be.

Excerpt from *Bob Vila's Guide to Buying Your Dream House* (Boston: Little, Brown, 1990).

Check Your Comprehension

1. How is home ownership related to "The American Dream"?

2. Why is the percentage of people owning their own homes decreas-
ing in the United States?

3. Why are younger buyers more disadvantaged now than older buyers
were when it comes to buying a home?

Vocabulary: Housing Terminology

Refer to the reading to determine the meanings of the following phrases. Then match the phrases to their definitions:

_____ 1. down payment

_____ 2. principal

_____ 3. mortgage

_____ 4. foreclosure

_____ 5. interest

a. when the lender revokes the rights to a property because the owner was unable to pay for it

b. an agreement to borrow money in order to buy a house

c. a portion of the house price that must be paid in advance

d. the actual sum of money lent, which must be repaid along with other fees

e. a percentage on the total amount of money borrowed, which must be paid back along with the original money borrowed

Think About It

1. The author implies that Americans think of home ownership as uniquely American. Do you agree? Why or why not?

2. What are the attitudes or policies about home ownership in your own country?

3. Think about the advantages and disadvantages of owning your own home. Why would you like to have your own home? Why wouldn't you? Fill in the table below, and then, based on your reasons, try to convince a partner why you would (or wouldn't) want a house.

Advantages	Disadvantages

Before You Read

Figure 1.1   American Mobility

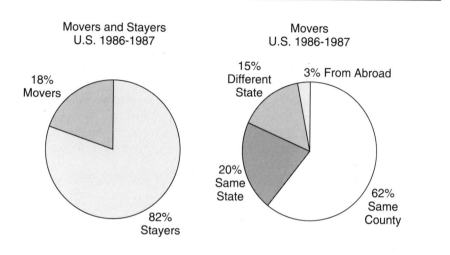

Source: Bureau of the Census, *Statistical Abstract of the United States, 1989* (Washington, D.C., 1989), table 25.

In this reading, the author discusses a common event in many Americans' lives—selling their homes and moving.

Before you read, think about the following questions:

* Have you or your family ever moved to a new home? What was the experience like?

* What is the difference between a "house" and a "home"?

About the Author

Andy Rooney began his writing career as a correspondent for *The Stars and Stripes*, a military newspaper, during World War II. He has since written for television and many newspapers. He is currently well known for his short, humorous weekly contribution to the television news program *Sixty Minutes*.

Home

by Andy Rooney

One Saturday night we were sitting around our somewhat shop-worn living room with some old friends when one of them started try-ing to remember how long we'd lived there.

"Since 1952," I said. "We paid off the mortgage eight years ago."

5   "If you don't have a mortgage," he said, "the house isn't worth as much as if you did have one."

Being in no way clever with money except when it comes to spend-ing it, this irritated me.

"To whom is it not worth as much," I asked him in a voice that was
10   louder than necessary for him to hear what I was saying. "Not to me, and I'm the one who lives here. As a matter of fact, I like it about fifty percent more than I did when the bank owned part of it."

"What did you pay for it?" he asked.

"We paid $29,500 in 1952."

15   My friend nodded knowingly and thought a minute.

"I'll bet you," he said, "that you could get $85,000 for it today . . . you ought to ask $95,000."

I don't know why this is such a popular topic of conversation these days, but if any real estate dealers are reading this, I'll give them some
20   money-saving advice. Don't waste any stamps on me with your offers to buy. You can take me off your mailing list.

Our house is not an investment. It is not a hastily erected shelter in which to spend the night before we rise in the morning to forge on far-ther west to locate in another campsite at dusk. Our house is our home.
25   We live there. It is an anchor. It is the place we go to when we don't feel like going anyplace.

We do not plan to move.

The last census indicated that forty million Americans move every year. One out of every five packs up his things and goes to live some-
30   where else.

Where is everyone moving to? Why are they moving there? Is it really better someplace else?

If people want a better house, why don't they fix the one they have?

If the boss says they're being transferred and have to move, why
35   don't they get another job? Jobs are easier to come by than a home. I can't imagine giving up my home because my job was moving.

I have put up twenty-nine Christmas trees in the bay window of the living room, each a little too tall. There are scars on the ceiling to prove it.

40   Behind the curtain of the window nearest my wife's desk, there is a vertical strip of wall four inches wide that has missed the last four coats of paint so that the little pencil marks with dates opposite them would not be obliterated. If we moved, someone would certainly paint that patch and how would we ever know again how tall the twins were when they were four?

45   My son Brian has finished college and is working and no longer lives at home, but his marbles are in the bottom drawer of his dresser if he ever wants them.

There's always been talk of moving. As many as ten times a year we talk about it. The talk was usually brought on by a leaky faucet, some
50   peeling paint, or a neighbor we didn't like.

When you own a house you learn to live with its imperfections. You accommodate yourself to them and, like your own shortcomings, you find ways to ignore them.

Our house provides me with a simple pleasure every time I come
55   home to it. I am welcomed by familiar things when I enter, and I'm warmed by some ambience which may merely be dust, but it is our dust and I like it. There are reverberations of the past everywhere, but it is not a sad place, because all the things left undone hold great hope for its future.

60   The talk of moving came up at dinner one night ten years ago. Brian was only half listening, but at one point he looked up from his plate, gazed around the room and asked idly, "Why would we want to move away from home?"

When anyone asks me how much I think our house is worth, I just
65   smile. They couldn't buy what that house means to me for all the money in both local banks.

The house is not for sale.

Excerpt from Andy Rooney, *And More by Andy Rooney* (Warner Books, 1983).

Check Your Comprehension

1.   What is the author's definition of "home"?

2.   Why does he say that he does not want to move?

3.   What is the significance of the "little pencil marks with dates" (line 41)?

Vocabulary: Two-Word Verbs

Choose the correct verb phrase for each of the sentences below. You may have to change the form of the verb (add -s, -ed, etc.). Note that the verb and the preposition may be separated in some sentences.

pay off	pay for	take off	put up	bring on
give up	come up	move away	pack up	come by

1. I need to _____ my debts _____ before I buy a new house.

2. If you move out of your house, you should _____ your

   name _____ the mailbox.

3. Before leaving, he _____ his belongings.

4. Beatrice _____ her new furniture with a credit card.

5. In general, you should not _____ your old apartment before you find a new one.

6. We couldn't afford to move, so we _____ with some new ideas for redecorating our house.

7. My father always _____ the holiday decorations

   _____ every December.

8. My daughter was sad when we had to _____ from our old house.

9. You don't _____ a good house every day—you should buy that one immediately!

10. I don't know what _____ his anger _____.
    Maybe he's tired of his noisy neighbors.

Think About It

1. In line 35, the author claims that new jobs are easier to get than new homes. Do you agree?

2. What effect do you think high mobility has on a culture or community?

3. Does your first language have different words for *house* and *home?* Write a paragraph explaining the difference between these two words.

4. On the next page are five classified advertisements for houses for sale. Try to determine what the abbreviations in the ads mean by choosing the correct house(s) for each of the ten questions.

a.
AMESBURY, Prestigious Highlands area lovely 3 BR Col., new fully applc. kit., new electric, hdwd. flrs., deck, nat'l woodwork, full bsmt., built-in hutch in DR. $175K.

b.
CONCORD, Lovely 10 rm., 5 BR, 2½ bath Garr. Col. on cul-de-sac w/2.8 acres, slate foyer opens up to lg. LR w/frpl., library/study. DR & lg FR. $495K.

c.
HAVERHILL, Quality Condex, priv. fenced yard, pressure treated deck, lg. kit., abundant cbnt. space, 1½ baths, 2 BRs, bsmt. $89,500.

d.
READING, Surrounded by flowering shrubs & trees this lovely mint cond. home has 4 BRs, 2 baths, formal DR, sunrm. & very priv. pool area. $319,900.

e.
WAKEFIELD, Well maintained Col. in great loc. Dynamite kit., frpl. LR, hdwd. flrs., 2 car gar., central air & ingrd. pool. $189,900.

	a.	b.	c.	d.	e.
1. Which house is the cheapest?	___	___	___	___	___
2. Which house is the most expensive?	___	___	___	___	___
3. Which house(s) have wood floors?	___	___	___	___	___
4. Which house(s) have a fireplace?	___	___	___	___	___
5. Which house has the most bedrooms?	___	___	___	___	___
6. Which house(s) are in the Colonial style of architecture?	___	___	___	___	___
7. Which house(s) have a sunroom?	___	___	___	___	___
8. Which house(s) have a formal dining room?	___	___	___	___	___
9. Which house(s) have a two-car garage?	___	___	___	___	___
10. Which house(s) have a lot of cabinet space?	___	___	___	___	___

Synthesis

Discussion and Debate

1. Some people might claim that Americans are too "status" conscious; that is, money and possessions are too important to them. Do you agree? Why or why not? Do you think only Americans are too concerned with money?

2. Although Americans have a reputation for being materialistic, there is also a tradition in the United States of charity, or donating money or possessions to people who need it. (In 1987, $93.7 billion was donated to charity. This is the equivalent of $375 for every man, woman, and child in the country.) Does this statistic surprise you? How can the qualities of materialism and charity co-exist? Does your own culture have the same tradition of charity?

3. There are two very different ways of handling money: one is to spend it when you get it; the other is to save as much as you can. Do you deal with money in one of these ways? Is one way better than the other? What kind of attitude lies behind each?

4. Think of an additional question to ask your classmates about something in this chapter. (Ask for their ideas or opinions rather than specific information from the reading.)

Writing Topics

1. Does this chapter present any ideas or opinions with which you strongly agree or disagree? Write a paragraph about that idea.

2. Write a letter to a friend in your home city describing the home and possessions of an American you have met. (If you have not met any Americans yet, you can "invent" one to write about.)

3. Before visiting a new place, most people have certain beliefs about that place, perhaps from reading or from speaking to others about it. However, after they arrive, they may find a different situation from what they expected. Write a short essay explaining what you thought the United States would be like before you arrived. Then describe the things that were the same as you expected and the things that were different.

On Your Own

1. A primary way to motivate people to spend their money is through advertising. Look through some popular magazines or newspapers published in the United States, and find some advertisements for three different products. Examine the ads and determine to whom the advertisers are trying to appeal. Use the following questions to help you.

   • Are there any people pictured in the ad? If so, what sort of people (young, old, single, couple, etc.)?

   • Does the ad use a lot of writing? What kinds of words does it use to describe the product?

   • What magazine did you find it in? Who reads that magazine?

   • Do certain words appear in all the ads?

   Share your ads and ideas with your classmates.

2. Conduct a survey of U.S.-born Americans about the following topics. Speak to at least ten people. Summarize your results in writing. Here are some questions you can use:

   • How many times have you moved from one house to another in your lifetime?

   • How old are you?

   • How much money do you need to be "rich"?

   • How many of the following items do you or your family own?

   cars _____ (write number)

   television sets _____

   video cassette recorders _____

   computers _____

   Compare your results with your classmates'. Are there any differences? If so, why do you think those differences arose?

3. The film *Lost in America,* written and directed by Albert Brooks, provides a humorous illustration of the values represented in this chapter. Rent the videotape at a local video store and watch it. What are the values represented in the film as they relate to housing? To money? To mobility?

4. Interview someone who has made a major purchase recently (for example, a house, a car, or a boat). Ask about his or her experience. How did the salesperson treat him or her, both before and after the purchase was made? How did it feel to spend so much money? Was it a happy or an unhappy experience?

2
Name, Rank, and Serial Number

PART ONE
Name and Shape

Before You Read

Table 2.1   Fifty Common American Names

Female Name	Origin	Meaning
Anne	Hebrew	Graceful one
Barbara	Latin	Stranger
Carol	Latin	Strong and womanly
Catherine	Greek	Pure one
Christine	French	Christian
Cynthia	Greek	The moon
Deborah	Hebrew	The bee
Diana	Latin	Goddess
Donna	Italian	Lady
Elizabeth	Hebrew	Consecrated to God
Helen	Greek	Light, truth
Jane	Hebrew	God is gracious
Jennifer	Welsh	White phantom
Jessica	Hebrew	Wealthy
Julia	Latin	Youthful
Laura	Latin	Crown of laurel leaves
Linda	Spanish	Beautiful
Mary	Hebrew	Bitterness
Melissa	Greek	Honey
Patricia	Latin	Noble one
Rebecca	Hebrew	Bound
Sarah	Hebrew	Princess
Susan	Hebrew	Graceful lily
Theresa	Greek	Keeper
Victoria	Latin	Victory

Male Name	Origin	Meaning
Andrew	Greek	Strong, manly
Benjamin	Hebrew	Son of the right hand
Brian	Celtic	Strength and virtue
Charles	Old German	Strong, manly
Christopher	Greek	Christ-bearer
Daniel	Hebrew	God is my judge
David	Hebrew	Beloved one
Edward	Old English	Prosperous guardian
Gregory	Latin	Watchman
James	Old Spanish	The supplanter
Jeffrey	Old French	Divinely peaceful
John	Hebrew	God is gracious
Lawrence	Latin	Laurel-crowned one
Mark	Latin	Warlike
Michael	Hebrew	Like god
Nicholas	Greek	Victorious
Patrick	Latin	Noble one
Paul	Latin	Little
Peter	Latin	Stone
Richard	Old German	Powerful ruler
Robert	Irish	Famous ruler
Steven	German	Crowned one
Thomas	German	A twin
Timothy	German	Honoring God
William	Old German	Resolute protector

In the next reading, the author discusses the effect that names may have on a person's personality. He does this by telling a story from his own experience.

Before you read, think about the following questions:

- Does your own name have a particular meaning?
- What are the traditions or typical processes for naming children in your own culture?

Glossary

tight end and linebacker   Positions on an American football team

alderman of the First Ward   Elected representative from the first political division in the city of Chicago

About the Author

Mike Royko is a writer and a regular columnist for the newspaper, the *Chicago Tribune*.

What's in a Name?

by Mike Royko

A young couple I know has been trying to choose a name for their first child, which will arrive soon. It hasn't been easy.

They don't want to name their baby after a relative, a famous person or themselves. They want something distinctive, but not unusual.

5   They asked if I had any suggestions, since I went through the same thing a couple of times. "If it is a boy," I said, "name him Bronko or Bruno."

The woman was appalled: "Why would I want to name a tiny child Bronko? Or Bruno?"

10   Because it's a tough world, and with a name like Bronko, he won't grow up to be a wimp.

"Why didn't you name your sons Bronko or Bruno?" she asked.

The fact is, I tried. When my first son was born, and I saw how big he was, I wanted to name him Bronko. With a name like Bronko Royko,

15   he would probably end up as a tight end or maybe a linebacker, get through college free, maybe turn pro and make a lot of money. I could cash in for ten percent as his agent.

I was half right. He grew big enough to be not only a tight end, but maybe a goal post.

20   However, I was overruled on his name. Instead of Bronko, he was tagged with David.

David is a fine name, but it doesn't have any mud or soot or coal dust on it. It's a clean, refined, sensitive name.

So what happened? There he stands today, about 6½ feet high, huge

25   arms, strong back, and not once in his life has he ever knocked anybody unconscious. Instead, he's a shrink, a musician and a scholar.

And as I explained to that couple, his name helped his career. Who'd go to a shrink named Bronko?

I wanted to name my second son Rocco Rico Royko. I figured he'd

30   wind up as alderman of the First Ward, or maybe a jukebox distributor. I was vetoed on that too.

"But if I have a son," the prospective mother said, "I'm not interested in his becoming tough or macho. We just want something nice, but distinctive."

35   They showed me one of those books of names to help parents make a choice. "It even has a list of the most popular names today," the husband said, "and a list of the names that were popular years ago, when you were a kid."

I looked at the list and wasn't surprised. Everybody I know has a
40   kid with a trendy name.

Girls are being named Heather, Jennifer, Jessica, Kimberly, Allison
and Melissa. Boys are being named Jason, Joshua, Christopher, Scott,
Mark and Jeffrey.

When I was a kid, I didn't know anybody named Heather or Joshua.
45   In my neighborhood, boys had solid, workmanlike names: Stanley, Wal-
ter, Albert, Henry or Joe. Girls had in-the-kitchen names like Mildred,
Dorothy, Helen, Eleanor, Bertha and Gertrude.

Today it's not unusual to find people with monikers like Heather
Potkowski, Kevin Bongorino or Danielle Goldberg. No wonder young
50   people grow up confused about who they are.

So I suggested that they go for an old-fashioned name, maybe
Gertrude, so they could call her Gert.

"I'm not going to name my daughter Gert," the woman said. "That's
awful."
55   I suggested Phoebe. But they didn't like that any better.

"If it's a girl," the husband said, "I'm kind of leaning toward Lisa."

I made a retching sound and warned them that by the year 2000, one
out of every five young females in America would be named Lisa. And
they would all marry guys named Mark. Better to call her Pearl, so she'll
60   stand out. And if it's a boy, Elmer.

"Elmer!" she cried. "That's horrible!"

As I was leaving, they were pondering Samantha. The wife said: "We
could call her Sam. That's cute."

I told them that if they wanted to give her a man's name, why not
65   just call her Horace and be done with it.

A name choice is a serious matter, and many people have been embarrassed by the label they're stuck with. I'm sure people remember the
famous case of Joe Crapp, who went to court to get his name changed.

The judge said: "I don't blame you for wanting a new name, Joe.
70   What have you chosen?"

And Joe Crapp responded: "I want my name changed to John Crapp.
I'm tired of people always saying: 'Whaddaya know, Joe?'"

From the *Chicago Tribune*, June 4, 1987.

Check Your Comprehension

1. Why did the author want to name his own son Bronko or Bruno? Why didn't he give him one of those names?

2. Why didn't the author's friends like his suggestions for names for their baby?

3. According to the author, what is wrong with "trendy" names?

Vocabulary: Synonyms

Substitute one of the words or phrases from the list below for the italicized words in sentences 1–10. You may have to change the verb form.

a. cash in on	e. shrink	h. trendy
b. end up with	f. stand out	i. turn pro
c. go through	g. tagged with	j. veto
d. macho		

1. If you want to (*be different*) _____, an unusual name may help.

2. Emily is a (*fashionable*) _____ name.

3. The name Rocco might seem (*tough and masculine*) _____ to some people.

4. My husband wanted to name our baby "Jasper," but I (*rejected*) _____ the idea.

5. The name Bronko might not be advantageous for a (*psychiatrist*) _____ .

6. Gertrude was (*given*) _____ her old-fashioned name by her grandmother.

7. Many children of movie stars try to (*profit from*) _____ their famous names.

8. After winning the Olympic gold medal, many skaters (*become professionals*) _____ .

9. Mary Louise (*has*) _____ two names because her parents couldn't agree on only one.

10. I would not want to (*experience*) _____ my life with the name "Bonzo."

Think About It

1. Many writers and movie stars adopt pseudonyms—that is, names that they think sound better for their profession. For example, the real name of the famous actor John Wayne was Marion Morrison. Imagine you are a movie actor or writer and the company you work for wants you to change your name. Would you do it? Why or why not? If you would, what new name would you choose?

2. Write a short paragraph describing how you got your name and what it means.

3. The table at the beginning of this section lists the formal versions of 50 common names. However, many Americans choose to go by a "nickname," a shortened or changed form of their full name. Below is a list of standard nicknames. Can you determine what the formal version of each nickname is? (There may be more than one nickname for the same name.)

FEMALE NICKNAME	FORMAL NAME	MALE NICKNAME	FORMAL NAME
Susie	_____	Nick	_____
Sally	_____	Larry	_____
Betty	_____	Tom	_____
Jenny	_____	Ed	_____
Debbie	_____	Chuck	_____
Liz	_____	Dave	_____
Patty	_____	Jeff	_____
Laurie	_____	Greg	_____
Cathy	_____	Ben	_____
Missy	_____	Jim	_____
Vicky	_____	Dick	_____
Kay	_____	Bill	_____
Beth	_____	Ted	_____
Becky	_____	Jack	_____
Sue	_____	Mike	_____
Terry	_____	Pat	_____
Katie	_____	Bob	_____
Pat	_____	Steve	_____
Chris	_____	Andy	_____

Before You Read

Table 2.2   Ideal Weight

Height		Weight in Pounds	
Feet	Inches	Men	Women
4	10	—	102–131
4	11	—	103–134
5	0	—	104–137
5	1	—	106–140
5	2	128–150	108–143
5	3	130–153	111–147
5	4	132–156	114–151
5	5	134–160	117–155
5	6	136–164	120–159
5	7	138–168	123–163
5	8	140–172	126–167
5	9	142–176	129–170
5	10	144–180	132–173
5	11	146–184	135–176
6	0	149–188	138–179
6	1	152–192	—
6	2	155–197	—
6	3	158–202	—
6	4	162–207	—

Source: Metropolitan Life Insurance Company Height and Weight Tables, 1983.

The author of this essay discusses fatness and thinness from an unusual perspective. She uses a lot of descriptive vocabulary that may be difficult to understand at first. Try to read the essay the first time without using your dictionary.

Before you read, think about the following questions:

* How are overweight people regarded in your culture?
* Do you have any stereotypes about the behavior of overweight people?

Glossary

> *S&H Green Stamps*   Stamp that is given for each dollar spent (but only in some states and in some stores) and that can be traded for merchandise

About the Author

Suzanne Britt is the author of *Skinny People Are Dull and Crunchy Like Carrots*. She teaches English at Meredith College in North Carolina.

That Lean and Hungry Look
by Suzanne Britt

Caesar was right. Thin people need watching. I've been watching them for most of my adult life, and I don't like what I see. When these narrow fellows spring at me, I quiver to my toes. Thin people come in all personalities, most of them menacing. You've got your "together"
5 thin person, your mechanical thin person, your condescending thin person, your tsk-tsk thin person, your efficiency-expert thin person. All of them are dangerous.

In the first place, thin people aren't fun. They don't know how to goof off, at least in the best, fat sense of the word. They've always got to
10 be adoing. Give them a coffee break, and they'll jog around the block. Supply them with a quiet evening at home, and they'll fix the screen door and lick S&H green stamps. They say things like "there aren't enough hours in the day." Fat people never say that. Fat people think the day is too damn long already.

15 Thin people make me tired. They've got speedy little metabolisms that cause them to bustle briskly. They're forever rubbing their bony hands together and eyeing new problems to "tackle." I like to surround myself with sluggish, inert, easygoing fat people, the kind who believe that if you clean it up today, it'll just get dirty again tomorrow.

20 Some people say the business about the jolly fat person is a myth, that all of us chubbies are neurotic, sick, sad people. I disagree. Fat people may not be chortling all day long, but they're a hell of a lot *nicer* than the wizened and shriveled. Thin people turn surly, mean, and hard at a young age because they never learn the value of a hot-fudge sundae
25 for easing tension. Thin people don't like gooey soft things because they themselves are neither gooey nor soft. They are crunchy and dull,

like carrots. They go straight to the heart of the matter while fat people let things stay all blurry and hazy and vague, the way things actually are. Thin people want to face the truth. Fat people know there is no
30 truth. One of my thin friends is always staring at complex, unsolvable problems and saying, "The key thing is. . . ." Fat people never say that. They know there isn't any such thing as the key thing about anything.

Thin people believe in logic. Fat people see all sides. The sides fat people see are rounded blobs, usually gray, always nebulous and truly
35 not worth worrying about. But the thin person persists. "If you consume more calories than you burn," says one of my thin friends, "you will gain weight. It's that simple." Fat people always grin when they hear statements like that. They know better.

Fat people realize that life is illogical and unfair. They know very
40 well that God is not in his heaven and all is not right with the world. If God was up there, fat people could have two doughnuts and a big orange drink anytime they wanted it.

Thin people have a long list of logical things they are always spouting off to me. They hold up one finger at a time as they reel off these
45 things, so I won't lose track. They speak slowly as if to a young child. The list is long and full of holes. It contains tidbits like "get a grip on yourself," "cigarettes kill," "cholesterol clogs," "fit as a fiddle," "ducks in a row," "organize," and "sound fiscal management." Phrases like that.

They think these 2,000-point plans lead to happiness. Fat people
50 know happiness is elusive at best and even if they could get the kind thin people talk about, they wouldn't want it. Wisely, fat people see that such programs are too dull, too hard, too off the mark. They are never better than a whole cheesecake.

Fat people know all about the mystery of life. They are the ones
55 acquainted with the night, with luck, with fat, with playing it by ear. One thin person I know once suggested that we arrange all the parts of a jigsaw puzzle into groups according to size, shape, and color. He figured this would cut the time needed to complete the puzzle by at least 50 percent. I said I wouldn't do it. One, I like to muddle through. Two, what
60 good would it do to finish early? Three, the jigsaw puzzle isn't the important thing. The important thing is the fun of four people (one thin person included) sitting around a card table, working on a jigsaw puzzle. My thin friend had no use for my list. Instead of joining us, he went outside and mulched boxwoods. The three remaining fat people
65 finished the puzzle and made chocolate, double-fudged brownies to celebrate.

The main problem with thin people is they oppress. Their good intentions, bony torsos, tight ships, neat corners, cerebral machinations, and pat solutions loom like dark clouds over the loose, comfortable,
70 spread-out, soft world of the fat. Long after fat people have removed

their coats and shoes and put their feet up on the coffee table, thin people are still sitting on the edge of the sofa, looking neat as a pin, discussing rutabagas. Fat people are heavily into fits of laughter, slapping their thighs and whooping it up, while thin people are still politely 75 waiting for the punch line.

Thin people are downers. They like math and morality and reasoned evaluation of the limitations of human beings. They have their skinny little acts together. They expound, prognose, probe, and prick.

Fat people are convivial. They will like you even if you're irregular 80 and have acne. They will come up with a good reason why you never wrote the great American novel. They will cry in your beer with you. They will put your name in the pot. They will let you off the hook. Fat people will gab, giggle, guffaw, gallumph, and gossip. They are generous, giving, and gallant. They are gluttonous and goodly and great. What 85 you want when you're down is soft and jiggly, not muscled and stable. Fat people know this. Fat people have plenty of room. Fat people will take you in.

From *Newsweek Magazine*, October 9, 1978.

Check Your Comprehension

1. What qualities does the author seem to value in other people?

2. What "evidence" does the author supply to show that fat people are nicer than thin people?

3. How does the author feel about "truth" and "logic"?

Vocabulary: Adjectives — Negative and Positive

Each of the following adjectives describes a human quality. Find each of these vocabulary items in the text, and then decide from the context whether the author uses it as a positive adjective, a negative adjective, or a neutral one. Place a + in the blank before the word if it is positive, a − if it is negative, and a ∅ if it is neutral. Then use each word in a sentence showing you know the meaning of the word. Write your sentences in the blanks numbered 1–10.

_____ neurotic	_____ gallant
_____ gooey	_____ gluttonous
_____ surly	_____ sluggish
_____ menacing	_____ easygoing
_____ jolly	_____ convivial

1. _____

_____

2. _____

_____

3. _____

_____

4. _____

_____

5. _____

_____

6. _____

_____

7. _____

_____

8. _____

_____

9. _____

_____

10. _____

_____

Think About It

1. Do you agree with the author's opinion about fat people? Why or why not?

2. Do you think a person's size has anything to do with his or her personality? If so, how? If not, why not?

3. Imagine you are going to write a response to Britt's article, arguing the opposite point of view—that thin people are "superior" to overweight people.

   (i) Fill in the following chart with adjectives describing each type of person (fat, thin). (Remember, you do not really have to believe that these adjectives describe the truth.)

	Thin Person	Fat Person
Example:	energetic	lazy

   (ii) Prepare your response (either orally or in writing) based on your chart.

PART TWO
Age: Only as Old as You Feel

Before You Read

Figure 2.1   Life Expectancy in the United States

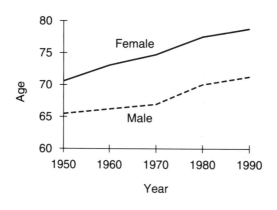

The author of this article describes how she feels when her parents decide to retire and move away.

Before you read, think about the following questions:

- Have your parents or grandparents retired? How did you feel about it? How did they feel about it?

- How is retirement treated in your culture? (At what age do people retire? What do they do after their retirement?)

Glossary

L.I.   Long Island, a residential island of New York State, near New York City

Margaret Mead   Twentieth-century American anthropologist whose research focused on family and social structures

About the Author

Randi Kreiss is a writer who lives in New York.

Bittersweet Farewell of a Grown-Up Child

by Randi Kreiss

My parents have retired to Florida, and I am suffering an empty nest syndrome. They taught me the value of family, urged me to settle in town, nurtured the love of my children and then they left. I may be 31 years old and a liberated woman, but it still hurts. There are thousands
5 of people like me, experiencing a kind of delayed separation anxiety. Our parents are leaving the old hometown and shaking our roots loose as they go.

In a parody of their ancestors who endured an arduous sea voyage in hopes of a better life, my well-heeled, lively parents tooled down I-95
10 in search of sunny days and four for bridge. They traded their snow shovels for golf clubs and left us behind to cope with real life.

Part of me is happy for them. Both in their 50's, fit and independent, they have made a gutsy move. Methodically, they lightened their load, sold their house and my father's dental practice, and bought an apart-
15 ment in Florida.

But somewhere inside, I'm uneasy. Certainly my own life, my husband's life and my children's lives are diminished by their absence. The daily calls or visits or just sightings of my mother's car parked in town were like touching down for a moment, a warm spot in each day. There
20 were always noncritical ears to hear my side of an argument, a sensible voice to advise compromise. Mainly, the balance they provided on a daily basis is missing, the balance between past and present and the balance between my identity as a child and as a mother. That is all gone, because phone communication is brief and all the news is edited. The
25 daily aches, fears and squabbles are deleted. Good news only, kids, it's Grandma calling.

I wonder about two active people retiring. What will they do for the next 30 or 40 years? Can they really withdraw from the tumult of Northern life and embrace Southern ways? Or are they just exchanging one
30 set of anxieties for another? Perhaps this is self-centered—I may be unwilling to see my parents retire because it is another confirmation that I, too, am getting older.

There is anger in me as well. The child inside is holding her breath and turning blue; an unreasonable reaction, but let me explain.
35 We live in a lovely community where people don't grow up longing to find a better life for themselves. They long to be able to afford this one, right here.

My parents, sisters, and I lived in our house in Cedarhurst, L.I., for

most of our lives. Not that we were overprotected, but I wouldn't sleep
40 at a friend's house until I was 14. When it came time to go "away" to
college, I only made it as far as New York University.

Of course, I married the boy I knew in high school, and we settled
just down the road in Woodmere. Only my sister threatened our geo-
graphic unity. Always the independent one (she made it to Boston for
45 college), she married and settled in Philadelphia.

I began making phone calls to her. "What if you both get a virus in
the middle of the night?" I whispered. "What happens when you have a
baby and Mom isn't there to help out?"

After three years, they moved just down the road to Hewlett. So
50 there we were, all settled in, reveling in our togetherness, except Mom
and Dad, apparently. They smiled lovingly at us all and announced their
impending retirement.

I'm the first one to admit it was childlike, but I was angry. My father
was always quoting Margaret Mead on the value of an extended family.
55 Now he wanted to deprive his grandchildren of that experience.

Once the decision was made, my parents began shedding possessions as a dog shakes out fleas. For my husband and me, the house was
part of our youth and romance. Memories mixed with the dust and plaster as pictures came down and relics were hauled up from the basement.
60 We all thought it would be fun to have a garage sale on the last
weekend before they moved. Bits and pieces of ourselves, our old life
together, were strewn about the garage waiting for buyers. But the day
was cold and traffic was slow. By afternoon, my father stood outside
alone, handing our things to strangers.
65 Maybe part of the sadness was the air of finality. There were un-
mentioned but strongly felt parallels to the cleaning out and closing up
that accompanies a death. My parents vacuumed up every trace of
themselves, and they left town.

The woman in me shouts "bravo" for their daring and the new days
70 before them. They didn't wait for widowhood or illness to force their
retirement. They made a free choice.

But there is still the child in me, too, perhaps more petulant in this
time of adjustment.

Several months ago, the night before my husband and I left for a
75 vacation alone, I heard my 4-year-old daughter crying in bed. She didn't
want us to go, she said. Patiently, logically, I explained that mothers and
fathers need time away to themselves. She nodded her head, endured
my explanation and asked, "But who will be my mother when you're
gone?"
80 When we said goodbye to my parents, the child in me was asking
the same question.

From the *New York Times*, March 22, 1979.

Check Your Comprehension

1. What was the author's family life like?

2. Why is the author upset that her parents are moving to Florida?

3. What passages in this reading tell you that the author may have been "overprotected" by her parents?

Vocabulary: Defining Words from Context

Write explanations or definitions of the italicized words or expressions in the following passages, taken from the reading. Use the information in the passage to help you.

1. My parents have retired to Florida, and I am suffering an *empty nest syndrome.*

   empty nest syndrome: _____

   _____

   _____

   _____

2. In a *parody* of their ancestors who endured an arduous sea voyage in hopes of a better life, my *well-heeled*, lively parents *tooled down* I-95 in search of sunny days and four for bridge.

   parody: _____

   _____

   _____

   _____

   well-heeled: _____

   _____

   _____

   _____

   tooled down: _____

   _____

   _____

   _____

3. The daily calls or visits or just sightings of my mother's car parked in town were like *touching down* for a moment, a warm spot in each day.

   touching down: _____

   _____

   _____

   _____

4. Memories mixed with the dust and plaster as pictures came down and *relics* were hauled up from the basement.

   relics: _____

   _____

   _____

   _____

5. But there is still the child in me, too, perhaps more *petulant* in this time of adjustment.

   petulant: _____

   _____

   _____

   _____

Think About It

1. The author describes her feelings about her parents "leaving home." How is this different from the way parents feel when their children leave home?
2. The author emphasizes several times that her feelings are "childish." Do you agree? Why or why not?
3. Imagine that you are the author's parents. Write a letter to your daughter explaining why you want to retire and move to Florida.

Before You Read

Figure 2.2   The Aging of the Population: 1960 and 1987

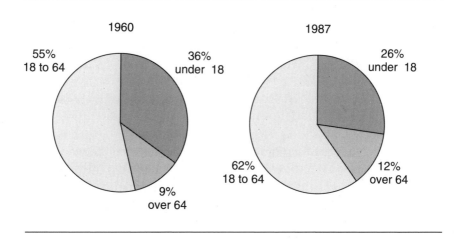

This essay deals with the idea of the "generation gap," the miscommunication between adults and the younger generation. It was written by an 18-year-old who expresses his opinions about adults' attitudes toward teenagers.

Before you read, think about these questions:

* How are teenagers treated by adults in your own culture?

* What prejudices do you think people have against you because of your age?

Glossary

Rousseau   French philosopher of the Enlightenment

Plato   Considered to be the most important ancient Greek philosopher

"Why Johnny Can't Read"   Title of a popular article discussing the failures of American education

Allan Bloom   Modern social critic and author of a popular book, *The Closing of the American Mind,* in which he argues that American education is in crisis

William Bennett   Former Secretary of Education, 1985–1988

The Enlightenment   Eighteenth century in Europe; called *The Enlightenment* because there was a new confidence in science and reason, and less reliance on religion and faith

SAT   Scholastic Aptitude Test; a general examination taken by high-school students planning to attend college

About the Author

Graham Charles wrote this essay when he was in high school. He is now a student at the University of California at Berkeley and plans to major in the dramatic arts.

A Teenager Talks Back

by Graham Charles

Imagine the average American adult walking down the average city street and seeing several average teenagers walk toward him. Brightly dressed, some are listening to suggestive music on portable stereos while others talk loudly about parties and recreational opportunities. 5 As an advocate of peace and quiet, the God-fearing grown-up feels intense disappointment and fear on seeing the "Future of America" personified, and may even display a contempt almost bordering on hatred. From where does this animosity come? Why are adults attacking *me,* the American teenager?

10   As I see it, it begins with the unflattering images of adolescents in the media. Television and movies portray teens as an alien race with below-average intelligence and an insatiable appetite for sex, drugs and rock music. Newspaper and magazine articles document our hideous

deficiencies in science, math and geography while pop-philosophy
15   books about the generally poor state of students' minds are marketed
to an all-too-hungry public by professors who spend more of their lives
with Rousseau and Plato than with the people they write about. These
books become best sellers, sucked in by adults-on-the-street who believe that young people constitute a separate species. This classifica-
20   tion is only reinforced by our style of dress and by our music.

The line between the generations is drawn; teenagers are sub-
human. Adults visualize us as drunk drivers, illiterate delinquents, punk
rockers in leather, and then judge every young person they meet by that
stereotype. They seem chilly when they deal with us; they keep their
25   distance and segregate us by age. And we begin to dislike them for with-
holding the right to their friendship. Such skirmishes drive a wedge between us, solidifying the sides of the battle. I propose a truce.

—First, adults must stop using studies designed to show how stupid we are. The statistics are fascinating, but they amount to little more
30   than teen bashing. Too many articles today are halfhearted attempts to
discover "why Johnny can't read," and barely disguise the perverse
pleasures taken in seeing how stupid Johnny can be. To know what we
do not know is only the starting point of an education, yet the most pub-
licized findings detail how many students cannot locate the United
35   States on a world map or say when Columbus landed in the New World.
Unfortunately, the real problem of what teachers do or do not teach us
is almost always glossed over.

—Adults should avoid the trap baited by Allan Bloom, William Bennett and the other overlords of education who take statistics from mis-
40   directed studies and use Enlightenment philosophy to attack teenagers.
As intellectual name-droppers, they blame kids for causing education's
problems. They deprecate teenage lifestyles in their books and at their
press conferences. We are ready targets: we sport easy-to-criticize
clothes and haircuts; we do not vote, and we have relatively little pur-
45   chasing power. Call us shallow, call us lazy, call us stupid, but adults
know there is little chance of retaliation. Using teenagers as scapegoats
is too easy.

—The ceaseless grading of students must be stopped. The various
numbers that are attached to us are not much different from astrological
50   forecasts: they *seem* about right, but they just don't fit the individual at
all. SAT scores and grade-point averages are only rough indicators of
our worthiness. But the need to get high numbers puts enormous pressure on us to achieve. "Successful" students get measurably more respect than underachievers, as well as scholarship money and their first
55   choice of colleges. Unfortunately, many work so hard to gain that il-
lusory image of success that they remain ignorant about the qualities
that are needed to be a successful human being.

The constant categorizing of students as successful or not only serves to strengthen the insidious process that treats teenagers as sta-
60 tistics, which, in turn, increases the pressure on them to distinguish themselves in some way. Eventually, the vicious cycle collapses, as do too many students.

Research should be devoted to improving education, not tearing students apart. Cut out these worthless surveys, as well as standardized
65 tests administered to bolster both school and state rankings; they are only depleting school budgets. Use the money to improve schools in the inner cities and to bring teachers' salaries up from the range of those who collect garbage.

I am not trying to blame all our problems on these heavily pub-
70 licized studies or the philosophers who have had a field day interpret-ing the portents for the future. Solving the education crisis cannot be done in 1,000 words. But America's fascination with teen bashing hurts. We are belittled while we are being studied. And I am simply tired of being talked about as a percentage and not as a person. Aside from our
75 parents and teachers, few adults even spend time with us.

To keep the truce, all adults must begin to talk to us. The infamous generation "gap" is caused less by grown-ups and teenagers not being able to talk to one another as by them not being willing to talk. Talk with a young person, not as one of "them," but as a person who just
80 happens to be young. Accept our strange ways and dress; then perhaps we will accept yours. Only by coming together will we be able to begin resolving our educational shortcomings. By pulling apart, we have only compounded them.

From *Newsweek*, October 24, 1988.

Check Your Comprehension

1. What is one reason the author thinks adults dislike teenagers?

2. Why does the author object to grades and tests?

3. What is the author's suggestion for improving relations between teens and adults?

Vocabulary: Words in Context

Write eight sentences using words from the columns below. Each sentence should include at least two words from two different columns. You may change the form of the verb but not of the nouns.

NOUN	VERB	MODIFIERS
animosity	reinforce	insidious
delinquents	segregate	perverse
scapegoat	bolster	insatiable
skirmish	deprecate	hideous
retaliation	criticize	worthless
surveys	publicize	halfhearted

Example: The *delinquents* were *segregated* from the rest of the population.

1. _____

_____

2. _____

_____

3. _____

_____

4. _____

_____

5. _____

_____

6. _____

_____

7. _____

_____

8. _____

_____

Think About It

1. Do you agree with the author that grades and tests should be abolished? Are there alternative methods of evaluating students that would work better?

2. Do you think the author's suggestion that adults and teenagers talk to each other will help solve the "generation gap"? How?

3. What are relationships between the generations like in your own culture?

4. "Dear Abby" is an advice column that appears in many newspapers. The following letter was written to Abby by a teenager. Read the letter and write a reply, advising the teenager how to solve her problems.

Dear Abby:

I am a fourteen-year-old girl and I hate my mother. It may sound terrible to you, but I really hate her. I used to think I would get over it, but now I know I never will.

Sometimes I think I will go out of my mind if she doesn't quit picking on me. I never do anything to suit her. She doesn't like my clothes, my hair, my friends, or anything.

My friends are not bums, either. They are good kids and my mother says they look like trash. They aren't.

Please help me, Abby, before I run away from home. I cry myself to sleep at night because my mother is so hateful. If I baby-sit, she makes me put the money in the bank. Other girls can buy records or do whatever they want with the money they earn.

Don't tell me to talk to my father. He's always on her side. And don't tell me my mother "loves" me and is only doing things for my own good. If you print my letter, don't sign my name or I'll get killed.

Miserable in Phoenix

From Abigail van Buren, *The Best of Dear Abby* (New York: Andrews & McMeel Inc., 1981).

Synthesis

Discussion and Debate

1. Some people argue that name, age, and size are superficial or unimportant. They say that it's important to know the "real" person. Do you agree? Why or why not?

2. In general, in the United States, it is considered impolite to ask an adult his or her age or weight. Are there any "taboo" questions like this in your culture?

3. Currently, plastic surgery is frequently used to make a person younger looking, thinner, or just more attractive. What is your opinion of this trend?

4. Think of another question to ask one of your classmates about the ideas and opinions presented in this chapter.

Writing Topics

1. If it were easy to change something about yourself—name, age, size, etc.—would you do so? What would you change? Write a paragraph explaining your answer.

2. Many people believe that certain "handicaps" make us "better" people. For example, Suzanne Britt thinks being fat makes you more fun and nicer; Mike Royko believes having a strange name will make you tougher. Have you (or someone you know) had some kind of "handicap"? Write one or two paragraphs describing that handicap and how it has changed your (or your friend's) life.

3. Write a short essay describing the "perfect" person. Include his or her age, size, and other details. If such a person existed, do you think you would like him or her?

On Your Own

1. Look through some magazines for advertisements that use human models. Try to find at least four different types of models—for example, a fat person, an old person, or an Asian person. Answer the following questions or give the information requested for each advertisement.
   a. Describe the age, race, and weight of the model.
   b. What product is he or she advertising?
   c. How is he or she dressed?
   d. What is the model doing in the ad?
   Do the ads you found reinforce stereotypes about certain types of people?

2. The following films deal with some of the topics of this chapter. Rent one from your local video store and watch it.

Fatso   *Babycakes*
Harold and Maude   *Big*

What was your opinion of the film you saw? Summarize it briefly and give your classmates a review of the film. Include the following information:
a. Who starred in the film?
b. Do you think the actors were good?
c. What did you think of the story? Was it realistic? Funny? Shocking?
d. Would you recommend the film to your classmates?

3. Ask at least ten U.S.-born Americans the following questions (record your answers):
a. Have you ever lied about your age?
b. Is the weight listed on your driver's license correct?
c. Is the height listed on your driver's license correct?
d. Do you know anyone who has had plastic surgery?
e. Have you ever gone on a diet to lose weight?

4. Many Americans may have had nicknames when they were children—not the standard nicknames found in the exercise earlier, but nicknames that had something to do with some quality they had or that made fun of their real names. For example, a short person might get the nickname "Shrimp." Find some people who had nicknames when they were children, and ask them to explain how they got that name and how they felt about it.

3

The Bare Necessities

PART ONE
Food: Food for Thought

Before You Read

Table 3.1   Ten Most-Liked and Least-Liked Foods among U.S. College Students

	Most Liked				Least Liked		
Rank	*Food*	*Rank*	*Food*	*Rank*	*Food*	*Rank*	*Food*
1	ice cream	6	orange juice	1	chicken livers	6	pickled beets
2	soft rolls	7	roast turkey	2	turnips	7	baked squash
3	beef steak	8	roast beef	3	sauteed liver	8	stewed tomatoes
4	hot biscuits	9	apple pie	4	fried eggplant	9	carrot-raisin salad
5	milk	10	fried chicken	5	cabbage	10	stewed rhubarb

Source: Adapted from M. A. Einstein and I. Hornstein, "Food Preferences of College Students and Nutritional Implications," *Journal of Food Science*, 35 (1970):429–35. Copyright held by Institute of Food Technologists.

The following passage discusses food preferences and manners and how they relate to ideas of social class in the United States.

Before you read, think about the following questions:

- Are there any American foods that you have discovered you particularly like? That you especially dislike?
- What foods from your own culture do you miss?

Glossary

Beef Wellington   Expensive cut of beef roasted with mushrooms inside a pastry shell

Eggs Benedict   Egg dish prepared with Canadian bacon, English muffins, and Hollandaise sauce

Blanquette de Veau   Dish of roasted veal

About the Author

Bernard Lyman received his doctorate in experimental psychology from Cornell University. He is an associate professor of psychology at Simon Fraser University, Burnaby, British Columbia, Canada.

A Psychology of Food
by Bernard Lyman

Although Americans like to think of themselves as a classless society, social mobility in the United States is largely constrained by table
manners, food preferences, and familiarity with various kinds of foods.
If we prefer meat loaf to lobster, we are thought to lack "class." If we
5   ask for corned beef hash or a macaroni-and-cheese casserole in an ex-
clusive restaurant, we embarrass our companions, and even though we
actually order Beef Wellington, the waiter snubs us or serves us conde-
scendingly for the rest of the evening. Anyone who likes liver is either
odd or anemic, and anyone who drinks buttermilk is thought to be
10   aging, dull, and constipated. A male who does not like steak or roast
beef is seen as somewhat less than red-blooded and would certainly be
considered a poor marriage risk by many girls' parents. Until recently,
one might have been taunted with ethnic slurs for liking Polish sausage,
provolone cheese, or catfish. Ethnic foods, however, have become
15   popular and chic, and many foods that were once considered déclassé
now appeal to people. In order to be socially correct, one must keep up
with these changes. Quiche is a bit passé, while the lowly pot roast may
be coming into vogue. We are expected to know a variety of fancy foods.
Only the unsophisticated would admit to being unfamiliar with Eggs
20   Benedict or Blanquette de Veau. Persons will go without wine in a restaurant rather than run the risk of being classed as gauche by making a
"mistake" in ordering or by ordering the wine they like rather than the
wine that is "right."

As adults, most of us spend at least two hours a day in eating or
25   preparing to eat. At no time is the thought of food far from our minds. If
thoughts of food are not initiated by hunger or habit, they are triggered
off by advertisements in magazines and newspapers and on radio and
television. The commercials either insist that we eat or assure us that
we will have heartburn, acid stomach, and the embarrassment of loose
30   dentures as a consequence of eating. By rights, psychiatrists' couches
should be sagging under the weight of clients seeking therapy for food-
induced neuroses.

Excerpted from Bernard Lyman, *A Psychology of Food* (New York: Van Nostrand Reinhold
Company, 1989).

Check Your Comprehension

1. Why might macaroni and cheese or corned beef hash be considered "lower class," while lobster or Beef Wellington are "high class"?

2. The author claims that a male who does not like roast beef or steak would be considered a "poor marriage risk" by many girls' parents. What does the author mean by this statement?

3. Why does the author say that he would expect many people to see psychiatrists because of food-induced problems?

Vocabulary: Foreign Words and Phrases

English contains many foreign words borrowed directly from other languages. Below are eight words from French and Italian found in this reading. Match each word with its correct definition.

_____ 1. macaroni	a. outdated
_____ 2. provolone	b. fashionable
_____ 3. chic	c. a cheese and egg dish
_____ 4. déclassé	d. style
_____ 5. quiche	e. noodles
_____ 6. passé	f. crude
_____ 7. vogue	g. low class
_____ 8. gauche	h. a white cheese

Think About It

1. Are any foods in your culture considered "low or high class"? What are they? Why do you think people think about food in this way?

2. The author states that Americans spend at least two hours each day eating or preparing to eat food. Is this time greater or less than the time spent in a day preparing and eating food in your culture?

3. It is well known that millions of people in the world are either starving or malnourished. Given this, what do you think about the "class consciousness" associated with food in developed countries?

4. This article points out that advertisements encourage us to eat more. Watch a half hour of television and count the number of food ads shown. Is the number higher or lower than you expected?

5. Survey at least ten American college students, asking them their ten most favorite foods and their ten least favorite. Combine your results with those of your classmates and construct a table like that shown above. How have the food preferences of U.S. college students changed since 1970? What hasn't changed?

Before You Read

Table 3.2   Weekly Expenditures for Food, 1986

Food at home	$37.73
Cereal and bread	5.29
Beef and pork	5.86
Poultry	3.16
Fish and eggs	1.79
Dairy products	4.82
Fruit and vegetables	6.14
Other	10.65
Food away from home	21.87
Total	$59.60

Source: Bureau of the Census, *Statistical Abstract of the United States, 1989* (Washington, D.C., 1989), table 709.

This reading discusses the unique contribution of American foods to the art of cooking. The author also discusses the contributions of different ethnic groups to what we know as "American" food.

Before you read, think about the following questions:

• What foods do you think of as being "American"?

• How has your own culture's cuisine contributed to the American diet?

About the Author

Jeff Smith has brought his cooking talents to millions of TV viewers in his weekly cooking show *The Frugal Gourmet.* In this program, he combines information about the history of food with instruction in cooking.

The Frugal Gourmet Cooks American
by Jeff Smith

We Americans have had a bad image of ourselves and our food for a long time, and I am done with it. I am so tired of people from the New World bowing to Europe, particularly France, when it comes to fine eating. We seem to think that if it comes from Europe it will be good, and if
5 it comes from America it will be inferior. Enough! We really do not understand our own food history, and I think that means we do not actually understand our own culture.

Most Americans do not think of themselves as an ethnic group, but we are an ethnic body, all of us put together. The word *ethnic* comes
10 from the Greek *ethnos*, meaning "nation." It refers not necessarily to a bloodline but to a group of persons distinguished by singular customs, characteristics, and language. While we are a nation populated for the most part by immigrants, we are nevertheless an ethnic group, a strange mixture, perhaps, but an ethnic group. We share a common language,
15 but more importantly we share a common memory. And there certainly is such a thing as American ethnic cooking. It is cooking that helps us remember and restore that common cultural memory.

All ethnic groups have foods that help them continue to identify themselves. Most of us Americans are not aware of the wonderfully
20 complex history of our own foods . . . since most of us still think that everything here came over from Europe or some other part of the world. The following is a list of food products that are ours, coming from one of the Americas, and these products were unknown in Europe prior to the discovery of the New World:

25 corn	sweet potatoes	tomatoes
turkey	vanilla beans	avocados
peanuts	potatoes	black walnuts
pimentos	lima beans	kidney beans
allspice	navy beans	bell peppers
30 squashes	pumpkins	string beans
cocoa	wild rice	cranberries

So there! These foods belong to us, and they actually do help define us. You enjoy turkey at Christmas even though your grandmother was born in Sicily. And the influence that these foods have had upon the rest of
35 the world should never be overlooked. Italy had no tomatoes, Ireland had no potatoes, and Switzerland had no vanilla or chocolate. Spain had no bell peppers or pimentos and China had no corn, peanuts, or sweet

potatoes. These last three edibles kept most of China alive at the beginning of the century. American foods have influenced the diet of the
40   world.

When thinking about who we are we must remember that America
was discovered by Europeans while on the search for food. Columbus
was not after property for housing developments, he was after trade
routes for valuable spices! And ever since the Europeans began moving
45   about between the New World and the Old there has been such a thing
as American ethnic food, food that is ours and is foreign to the rest of
the planet. You see, I am not talking about hamburgers and hot dogs,
though these are the delicacies that most Americans use in answering
the question about "real American food."

50   Our real American foods have come from our soil and have been
used by many groups—those who already lived here and those who
have come here to live. The Native Americans already had developed an
interesting cuisine using the abundant foods that were so prevalent.

The influence that the English had upon our national eating habits
55   is easy to see. . . . They were a tough lot, those English, and they ate in a
tough manner. They wiped their mouths on the tablecloth, if there happened to be one, and ate until you would expect them to burst. European travelers to this country in those days were most often shocked by
American eating habits, which included too much fat and too much salt
60   and too much liquor. Not much has changed! And, the Revolutionists
refused to use the fork since it marked them as Europeans. The fork
was not absolutely common on the American dinner table until about
the time of the Civil War, the 1860s. Those English were a tough lot.

Other immigrant groups added their own touches to the prepara-
65   tion of our New World food products. The groups that came still have a
special sense of self-identity through their ancestral heritage, but they
see themselves as Americans. This special self-identity through your
ancestors who came from other lands was supposed to disappear in
this country. The term *melting pot* was first used in reference to Amer-
70   ica in the late 1700s, so this belief that we would all become the same
has been with us for a long time. Thank goodness it has never worked.
The various immigrant groups continue to add flavor to the pot, all
right, but you can pick out the individual flavors easily.

The largest ancestry group in America is the English. There are
75   more people in America who claim to have come from English blood
than there are in England. But is their food English? Thanks be to God,
it is not! It is American. The second largest group is the Germans, then
the Irish, the Afro-Americans, the French, the Italians, the Scottish, and
the Polish. The Mexican and American Indian groups are all smaller
80   than any of the above, though they were the original cooks in this
country.

Some unusually creative cooking has come about in this nation because of all those persons that have come here. Out of destitution comes either creativity or starvation, and some of the solutions that the
85 new Americans have come up with are just grand. Only in America would you find an Italian housewife sharing recipes with her neighbor from Ireland. It has always been this way. The Native Americans were gracious enough to teach the first Europeans how to cook what was here, and we have been trading favorite dishes with one another ever
90 since.

I am talking about American food—food that has come to us from the early days, using American products, and that continues to provide one of the best diets on earth. I am not talking contemporary artsy plates, nor am I talking about *nouvelle gauche*. And, I am not talking
95 about meat loaf and lumpy mashed potatoes. Even at the time of the writing of the Declaration of Independence we were celebrating one of the most varied, and probably the best, cuisines in the world. It has not changed.

From Jeff Smith, *The Frugal Gourmet Cooks American* (New York: William Morrow & Co., 1987).

Check Your Comprehension

1. Why does the author state that all Americans belong to one ethnic group? How is this different from the usual meaning of ethnic group?

2. Why didn't many Americans use forks before the time of the Civil War?

3. What is meant by the term *melting pot* (line 69)?

4. What are the causes for the "unusually creative cooking" that the author says has come about in the United States?

Vocabulary: Outlining

The 21 items that the author lists as foods native to the Americas can be classified into groups. With the aid of a dictionary, determine what sort of food each is. Then complete the outline below with the names of these foods.

FOOD OF THE AMERICAS

I. Vegetables
    A. Beans
        1.
        2.
        3.
        4.
    B. Peppers
        1.
        2.
    C. Root vegetables
        1.
        2.
    D. Gourds
        1.
        2.

II. Fruits
     A. Berries
        1.
        2.
     B.
III. Nuts and spices
     A. Nuts
        1.
        2.
        3.
     B. Spices
        1.
        2.
IV. Cereals
     A.
     B.
V.   Meats
     A.

Think About It

1. Were you surprised to learn that any of the food listed on lines 25–31 originated in the Americas? Which ones?

2. Have any of these foods been incorporated into your own culture's cuisine? Which ones?

3. In general, what is your opinion of American food? What specific dishes do you like or dislike?

4. Below is a recipe for chocolate chip cookies, probably the most popular type of cookie in the United States. Look at the form of the recipe.

CHOCOLATE CHIP COOKIES

2¼ cups all-purpose flour
1 teaspoon baking soda
1 teaspoon salt
1 cup (two sticks) softened butter or margarine
¾ cup granulated sugar
¾ cup firmly packed brown sugar
1 teaspoon vanilla extract
2 eggs
1 12-ounce package (2 cups) chocolate chips

Preheat oven to 375 degrees Fahrenheit. In a small bowl, combine flour, baking soda and salt; set aside. In a large bowl, combine butter, sugar, brown sugar and vanilla extract; beat until creamy. Add eggs and beat. Gradually add flour mixture; mix well. Stir in chocolate chips. Drop by teaspoonfuls onto ungreased cookie sheets. Bake 8 to 10 minutes. Makes 100 cookies.

(i) What are the "rules" for writing a recipe? Complete the following statements.

a. The ingredients are listed _____

_____ .

b. The instructions use _____ sentences.

c. You must include information on these four things:

HINT: HINT:
_____ (oven)   _____ (time)

_____ (containers)   _____ (quantity)

(ii) What is one of your favorite foods (from your own or from American culture)? Write a recipe for that dish in the same format as the recipe above.

(iii) Explain to your classmates how to prepare this dish. Distribute copies of your recipe.

(iv) If you have kitchen facilities, make cookies according to the recipe above. Report in writing or to the class how difficult or easy it was. Were you successful? Bring samples to class for your classmates to taste.

PART TWO
Clothing: All Decked Out

Before You Read

Table 3.3   Money Spent Annually per Capita on Clothing, 1986

Age	Amount in dollars	Region of residence	Amount in dollars
Under 25	871	Northeast	1301
25–44	1375	Midwest	1116
45–64	1353	South	1049
65 and over	583	West	1202

Source: Bureau of the Census, *Statistical Abstract of the United States, 1989* (Washington, D.C., 1989), table 708.

This reading concerns the history of blue jeans and how this simple, working-class item of clothing has influenced fashion worldwide.

Before you read, think about the following questions:

• Do you own any blue jeans? When do you wear them?

• Why do you think blue jeans are so popular?

Glossary

James Dean, John Wayne, Marlon Brando   Movie stars popular in the middle part of the twentieth century

Jimmy Carter   39th president of the United States

Benelux nations   Belgium, the Netherlands, and Luxemburg

North Bronx   Section of New York City

About the Author

John Brooks is a writer who began his career as a contributing editor of *Time,* a weekly magazine, and who has also written for *The New Yorker.* He has written three novels, as well as several books on the cultural history of American business.

Dressing Down
by John Brooks

Beyond doubt, the jeans phenomenon is a seismic event in the history of dress, and not only in the United States. Indeed, the habit of wearing jeans is—along with the computer, the copying machine, rock music, polio vaccine, and the hydrogen bomb—one of the major contri-
5 butions of the United States to the postwar world at large.

Before the nineteen-fifties, jeans were worn, principally in the West and Southwest of the United States, by children, farmers, manual laborers when on the job, and, of course, cowboys. There were isolated exceptions—for example, artists of both sexes took to blue jeans in and
10 around Santa Fe, New Mexico, in the nineteen-twenties and -thirties; around 1940, the male students at Williams College took them up as a mark of differentiation from the chino-wearing snobs of Yale and Princeton; and in the late forties the female students of Bennington College (not far from Williams) adopted them as a virtual uniform, though only
15 for wear on campus—but it was not until the nineteen-fifties, when James Dean and Marlon Brando wore jeans in movies about youth in revolt against parents and society, when John Wayne wore them in movies about untrammeled heroes in a lawless Old West, and when many schools from coast to coast gave their new symbolism a boost by
20 banning them as inappropriate for classrooms, that jeans acquired the ideological baggage necessary to propel them to national fame.

After that, though, fame came quickly, and it was not long before young Americans—whether to express social dissent, to enjoy comfort, or to emulate their peers—had become so attached to their jeans that
25 some hardly ever took them off. According to a jeans authority, a young man in the North Bronx with a large and indulgent family attained some sort of record by continuously wearing the same pair of jeans, even for bathing and sleeping, for over eight months. Eventually, as all the world knows, the popularity of jeans spread from cowboys and anomic youths
30 to adult Americans of virtually every age and sociopolitical posture, conspicuously including Jimmy Carter when he was a candidate for the presidency. Trucks containing jeans came to rank as one of the three leading targets of hijackers, along with those containing liquor and cigarettes. Estimates of jeans sales in the United States vary wildly,
35 chiefly because the line between jeans and slacks has come to be a fuzzy one. According to the most conservative figures, put out by the leading jeans manufacturer, Levi Strauss & Company, of San Francisco, annual sales of jeans of all kinds in the United States by all manufacturers in 1957 stood at around a hundred and fifty million pairs, while

40 for 1977 they came to over five hundred million, or considerably more than two pairs for every man, woman, and child in the country.

Overseas, jeans had to wait slightly longer for their time to come. American Western movies and the example of American servicemen from the West and Southwest stationed abroad who, as soon as the Sec-
45 ond World War ended, changed directly from their service uniforms into blue jeans bought at post exchanges started a fad for them among Europeans in the late nineteen-forties. But the fad remained a small one, partly because of the unavailability of jeans in any quantity; in those days, European customers considered jeans ersatz unless they
50 came from the United States, while United States jeans manufacturers were inclined to be satisfied with a reliable domestic market. Being perennially short of denim, the rough, durable, naturally shrink-and-stretch cotton twill of which basic jeans are made, they were reluctant or unable to undertake overseas expansion.
55 Gradually, though, denim production in the United States increased, and meanwhile demand for American-made jeans became so overwhelming that in parts of Europe a black market for them developed. American jeans manufacturers began exporting their product in a serious way in the early nineteen-sixties. At first, the demand was greatest
60 in Germany, France, England, and the Benelux nations; later it spread to Italy, Spain, and Scandinavia, and eventually to Latin America and the Far East. By 1967, jeans authorities estimate, a hundred and ninety million pairs of jeans were being sold annually outside the United States; of these, all but a small fraction were of local manufacture, and
65 not imports from the United States, although American-made jeans were still so avidly sought after that some of the local products were blatant counterfeits of the leading American brands, complete with expertly faked labels. In the late nineteen-seventies, estimated jeans sales outside the United States had doubled in a decade, to three hundred
70 and eighty million pairs, of which perhaps a quarter were now made by American firms in plants abroad; the markets in Europe, Mexico, Japan, Australia, and other places had come so close to the saturation point that the fastest-growing jeans market was probably Brazil; Princess Anne, of Great Britain, and Princess Caroline, of Monaco, had been
75 photographed wearing jeans, and King Hussein of Jordan was reported to wear them at home in his palace; the counterfeiting of American brands was a huge international undertaking, which the leading American manufacturers combated with world-ranging security operations. In Russia, authentic American Levis were a black-market item regu-
80 larly commanding eighty or more dollars per pair. All in all, it is now beyond doubt that in size and scope the rapid global spread of the habit of wearing blue jeans, however it may be explained, is an event without precedent in the history of human attire.

From John Brooks, *Showing Off in America* (Boston: Little, Brown, 1981).

Check Your Comprehension

1. According to the author, what events caused jeans to become nationally popular?
2. What are some of the signs that indicate the popularity of jeans?
3. Why were European and other foreign countries so slow in adopting jeans as a popular style?

Vocabulary: Vocabulary in Context

Rewrite each sentence, paraphrasing the italicized word or phrase.

1. The jeans phenomenon is a *seismic event* (line 1) in the history of dress.

    _____

    _____

2. John Wayne wore jeans in movies about *untrammeled heroes* (line 18) in the lawless Old West.

    _____

    _____

3. Jeans acquired the *ideological baggage* (line 21) necessary to propel them to national fame.

    _____

    _____

4. The popularity of jeans spread from cowboys and *anomic youths* (line 29) to adult Americans.

    _____

    _____

5. European customers considered jeans *ersatz* (line 49) unless they came from the United States.

    _____

    _____

6. Some of the local products were *blatant counterfeits* (line 67) of the leading American brands.

    _____

    _____

Think About It

1. Three recent U.S. presidents—Jimmy Carter, Ronald Reagan, and George Bush—have been known for publicly wearing jeans. Can you think of any other world leaders who wear blue jeans? What do you think it says about American politicians in general?

2. Although blue jeans have been a popular fashion for decades, the style in which blue jeans are worn changes. For example, in the sixties baggy Levis were popular, in the seventies, tighter designer jeans. What is the current "style" of jeans?

3. How have blue jeans been accepted in your own culture? Who wears them? What types of places do they wear them to? How much do they cost?

4. Look through magazines or newspapers for advertisements for jeans. Try to find ads for three different brands of jeans. How do the ads differ? Which type would you be likely to buy, on the basis of the advertising? Bring your ads to class for discussion.

Before You Read

Table 3.4   Dress Code, Mumford High School, Detroit, Michigan

Not Permitted

Outer Garments

Garments which are in style and may endanger the health and safety of
    students
Leather coats and jackets
Sheepskin or animal-hide coats and jackets
Fur coats and jackets
Coats and jackets with fur collars
Jogging suits

Below-the-Waist Apparel

Expensive gym shoes or boots with snakeskin, lizard skin, leather, or other
    ornaments
Jeans and slacks with noticeable decorative ornaments, such as leather,
    snakeskin, etc.
Skirts more than two inches above the knee
Shorts of any kind or length
Tight-fitting jeans and slacks
High heels that exceed two inches

Table 3.4   (*Continued*)

Not Permitted

Jewelry

Neckwear, bracelets: gold or gold-plated, silver or silver-plated precious metal chains and/or ropes
Rings: more than one ring per hand; any ring more than a half inch (vertically and horizontally)
Large belt buckles: designer or custom-made, snakeskin, alligator, lizard skin, or seal skin
Briefcases: designer or custom-made, snakeskin, alligator, lizard skin, or sealskin
Glasses: designer glasses, such as Cazal, Emanuelle, Kahn, etc.
Designer jeans or leather-style matching outfits

Above-the-Waist and Full-Body Apparel

Any hat, sweatshirt, T-shirt, or apparel printed with a vulgar or obscene statement related to the use of drugs and/or alcohol
Halter tops
Fishnet and other transparent garments
Half-shirts
Tank tops
Suede and leather tops
Dark-tinted glasses
Unbuttoned shirts and blouses
Sweatbands
Scarves worn around the head
Bib overalls (straps not connected and hanging loosely from the shoulder)
Bedtime attire, such as rollers, pins, pajamas, and undershirts

Source: *Harper's Magazine*, September 1988.

The following article discusses the renewed interest in "dress codes" in public and private schools. During the 1960s, most schools did away with dress codes, and for many years students were allowed to wear what they wished. Now, these permissive dress codes are being revoked in many schools.

Before you read, think about the following questions:

- Did you have to adhere to a dress code or wear a uniform when you went to school? How did you feel about it then? How do you feel about it now?

- Do you think a dress code plays an important role in the effective administration of schools?

Glossary

school board   Group of citizens elected or appointed to make decisions affecting public schools

MTV   Music TV; a cable television channel that specializes in music videos

Lycra, Spandex   Types of cloth used to make tight, elastic clothing

Mohawk hairdo   Haircut made by shaving away all the hair except a band running down the center of the head; named after the Mohawk tribe of Native Americans

Hair*itage*   Play on the word "heritage," referring to the 1960s musical *Hair*

Crips and Bloods   Names of two youth gangs based in Los Angeles and well known for their violence and association with drugs

(look more like) Ike   Reference to President Dwight Eisenhower, 34th president of the United States and previously a U.S. army general and supreme commander of the allied forces in Europe during the Second World War; he was considered a conservative, during a time when dressing conservatively was popular.

About the Author

Tim Allis is a reporter for the magazine *People Weekly*.

Sloppy Duds Make Sloppy Minds
by Tim Allis

In Mundelein, Illinois, sixth-grader Kyle Lindblom was stopped by the principal of Carl Sandburg Middle School and forced to remove an earring—triggering a major re-evaluation of school rules. In Henry County, Georgia, dozens of high school students are engaged in what

5   the local papers call the Henry County Hair Wars—a face-off between long-locked males and a school board that has banned their trendy tresses. But on a steamy day at Roseville High in Mount Clemens, Michigan, students recently followed the dress code to the letter: Instead of wearing shorts, which are strictly forbidden, some wore skirts. Trouble

10   was, they were boys.

In other words, here we go again. The new school year, even as MTV stars flaunt the ratty-matty-fleecy-greasy *Hair*itage of the late '60s, has seen tighter dress regulations that look more like Ike.

"There are those who feel we tend to act the way we dress," says
15 Gary Marx, associate executive director of the American Association of School Administrators. "The school has become the place where the limits are being tested."

For the vigilant educators, no-nos range from the traditional (too-short skirts) to the outrageous (underwear worn as outerwear), with
20 innumerable variations in between: Lycra, ripped jeans, gold chains, cut-off jeans, tie-dyed shirts, see-through tops, Mohawk hairdos, and shaved heads. "We're constantly updating the list," says Roseville principal Curt Winnega. "I just added 'No spandex,' and I sent home a boy who had on a T-shirt that said I'M IN FAVOR OF ELIMINATING AIDS. I
25 WEAR A CONDOM. He came back wearing an Oxford cloth shirt. That's more like it."

Many students disagree. "I don't see how clothes affect your learning," says Roseville's Jennifer Carra, 17, who on a very hot day last June violated Winnega's "No tight shorts" rule and was sent home to change.
30 "I missed almost the whole hour. Now, *that* was disruptive." And many parents, themselves veterans of youthful protests, are siding with their kids: "If my son is almost old enough to be drafted, he can make his own decision about his hair," says Wilbur Lockhart, 45, owner of a supermarket in Jasper, Alabama, a community where parents and
35 students banded together to fight a Walker High School code.

Freedom of expression, however, is not the central issue in many schools. The big concern: Eliminate competition to be best-dressed. Baltimore schools, for example, have forbidden such high-priced apparel as animal skin jackets. And in Detroit, at least six elementary
40 schools have adopted voluntary uniforms.

The rags and regalia that end up on their hit lists, officials argue, can be more menacing than they look. Between 1983 and 1987 in Detroit, four boys were shot, two losing their lives, protecting their prized garb—leather jackets, jogging shoes, even a shirt that only looked like
45 silk. Detroit schools have since banned many popular labels. "There was just too much extortion and peer pressure," says Detroit Board of Education spokeswoman Marilyn Shreves. To curb high-tech high school drug dealing, a number of schools around the country have even outlawed accessories like message beepers. And in most L.A. schools,
50 bandannas are not allowed because they can symbolize gang affiliation, as can hats worn backwards or a preponderance of blue or red (the gang colors of the Crips and the Bloods).

Some argue that the pendulum is swinging so far toward conservative attire that drug-free and otherwise law-abiding kids are being
55 unjustly labeled. When Walker High School's new principal, Kenneth

Abbott, established his controversial ban on hair below the collar, a committee of parents petitioned the school board to compromise by allowing ponytails. "That way, the boys could take their hair down after school and still maintain self-respect," explains Judi Parnell, whose son
60 Brent, 15, was suspended with 36 others. No dice. When Abbott issued a warning, Brent got shorn. "It's not over," says Judi, who, with her contractor husband, Larry, and other parents, is considering legal action. "The school has won a battle, but not the war."

In the country's most dramatic showdown, Travis and Brian Wilkin-
65 son of Houston have stayed out of school since last October rather than shear their locks. Northbrook Senior High principal James King Jr. seems equally adamant about his ultimatum that the brothers cut their hair, which both wear halfway down their backs. "I have expected just two things from my sons: to act responsibly and to use good judgment,"
70 says their father, Dub, a close-cropped Vietnam veteran who runs a business-machine repair service from his home. "I don't hassle them about things like their hairstyles." Dub has raised Brian, 17, and Travis, 15, and their brother, Ray, 19, since he and the boys' mother divorced 10 years ago. To comply with Texas law, Brian and Travis are studying
75 at home. "I think I'm learning more this way," says Brian.

Last month Dub Wilkinson filed suit against the Spring Branch School District claiming the rule about his sons' hair length is unconstitutional because it is gender-based. "I just refuse to be the blunt instrument they use to beat my son over the head about a haircut,"
80 he says.

Such objections, though, have done little to sway school administrators. As Ed Parker, assistant superintendent of the Duncanville, Texas, school district, said: "We are seeking some form of government that brings back discipline and allows us to teach again."

From *People Weekly*, October 23, 1989.

Check Your Comprehension

1. What did the students do in reaction to the banning of shorts at Roseville High School in Michigan?

2. Many students disagree with the idea of dress codes. What arguments do they give in this article?

3. What are the reasons the school administrators give for needing dress codes?

4. Why do so many parents support their children, and not the schools, in this issue?

Vocabulary: Idioms and Colloquial Language

Find the following idioms in the reading. Determine what each might mean, and then write your own sentence, using each idiom correctly.

    a. to the letter (line 8)
    b. here we go again (line 11)
    c. that's more like it (line 25)
    d. hit lists (line 41)
    e. peer pressure (line 46)
    f. the pendulum is swinging (line 53)
    g. no dice (line 60)
    h. siding with (line 31)

Think About It

1. Did you have a dress code when you went to elementary or high school? What was it like?

2. Do you think that dress codes improve the educational environment? Why or why not?

3. Review the dress code of Mumford High School given at the beginning of this chapter. Does what you are wearing right now violate this dress code? Does any of your classmates' clothing? Which items do you think the school correctly bans students from wearing? Which items do you think are unreasonably banned?

4. A meeting of the school board: Imagine that you and your classmates live in a town whose school wants a dress code. With your classmates, hold a meeting of the school board to decide whether or not to institute this new, strict code. Some students should play members of the school board and school administrators; some, teachers; some, parents; and some, students. At the end of your meeting, everyone will vote on whether the dress code will be adopted as part of school policy.

Synthesis

Discussion and Debate

1. Some states in the United States tax food and clothing; some tax only clothing; some tax neither. Why do you think some states do not tax these items? Do you think these items should be taxed? Does your country tax any "necessities" of life?

2. Many expensive restaurants have "dress codes." What is the relationship between eating and dressing? Do you think that it is okay for restaurants to tell you how to dress?

3. Two proverbs in common use in the United States state "Clothes make the man" and "You are what you eat." What do these proverbs mean? Do you agree or disagree with them? Are there similar proverbs in your first language?

4. Think of an additional question to ask your classmates about the ideas and opinions presented in this chapter.

Writing Topics

1. Write a short review of a restaurant you have eaten in recently. What was the food like? How was the restaurant decorated? Was the service good?

2. Imagine your "ideal" night out. You can go to any restaurant you wish, and buy a new outfit to wear. Write a short essay explaining what restaurant or type of restaurant you will eat in, what you will wear, and what you will eat.

3. Go to a public place where people are eating (a cafeteria, a restaurant, a coffee shop) and observe the customers there. Select someone whose appearance you find interesting and write a brief description of his or her clothing, what this person is eating and drinking, and his or her general manners or behavior while eating. Is there a relationship between this person's appearance and his or her manners?

4. Write a short essay explaining how you believe American attitudes toward food and clothing are different from attitudes in your own culture.

On Your Own

1. Check your local television listings for television shows that give instruction in cooking (for example, *The Frugal Gourmet, The Great Chefs of New Orleans, The Great Chefs of Chicago, Julia Child and Company,* among many others). Report to the class on the show you watched.

2. Answer the following questions:

   • How much do you estimate you spend on clothing in one year?

   • How much do you estimate you spend on food in one week?

   Then ask at least three U.S.-born Americans the same questions. How similar to or different from their answers are yours? Compare your results with your classmates'.

3. Food and clothing, as well as being things influenced by fashion, are also necessities of life. Many Americans, especially at the holiday times of the year, donate packaged food and used clothing to families that need such help. Find out which agencies in your community (for example, the Salvation Army) accept donations of food or clothing for the poor.

   Report the following information to the class:

   Name of agency _____

   Address of agency _____

   _____

   Phone number _____

   What type of donations do they accept? _____

   _____

   When do they accept donations? _____

   _____

   If you are able to, make a donation to one of these agencies.

4

Friends and Relations

PART ONE
Family: The Ties That Bind

Before You Read

Figure 4.1   U.S. Marriage and Divorce Rates, 1960–1985

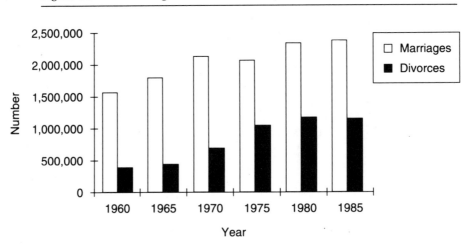

Source: Bureau of the Census, *Statistical Abstract of the United States* (Washington, D.C., 1989), table 127.

The following reading concerns the growing number of stepfamilies in the United States—families in which one or both parents have married a second time. This change is forcing us to re-examine whom we consider "family."

Before you read, think about the following questions:

• Are stepfamilies common in your own culture?

• How do you think most children react to new stepparents?

Glossary

Emerson   Ralph Waldo Emerson, an American poet and essayist

Led Zeppelin   Rock and roll band that became popular in the 1960s

Step by Step

by Barbara Kantrowitz and Pat Wingert

The original plot goes like this: first comes love. Then comes marriage. Then comes Mary with a baby carriage. But now there's a sequel: John and Mary break up. John moves in with Sally and her two boys. Mary takes the baby Paul. A year later Mary meets Jack, who is divorced
5 with three children. They get married. Paul, barely 2 years old, now has a mother, a father, a stepmother, a stepfather and five stepbrothers and stepsisters—as well as four sets of grandparents (biological and step) and countless aunts and uncles. And guess what? Mary's pregnant again.

This may sound like an unusually complicated family tree. It's not.
10 Some demographers predict that as many as a third of all children born in the 1980s may live with a stepparent before they are 18. According to the latest available Census figures, there were close to 7 million children living in stepfamilies in 1985, an increase of 11.6 percent in just five years. As startling as these statistics are, some experts think the
15 figures underestimate the number of children involved. For example, there's no way to accurately count youngsters in unofficial stepfamilies: homes where a child's biological parent is living with, but not married to, a new partner. Another group excluded by the Census is children who have stepsiblings or half-siblings in another household. These rela-
20 tionships have brought stepfamily ties to millions more homes. "Most people have a personal connection with a stepfamily," says University of Pennsylvania sociologist Frank Furstenberg. "If it's not their parents, it's their child or their grandparents or their husband's parents."

As their numbers grow in the next few decades, stepfamilies will
25 become even more prominent. Demographers expect that half of all people entering first marriages in the 1970s and 1980s will eventually divorce. The majority of them will probably remarry. "We will all have to work toward changing our internal maps of what a family should be," says Mala Burt, a Baltimore family therapist and president of the Step-
30 family Association of America, a 10-year-old group with 60 chapters in 17 states. All kinds of institutions, from schools to hospitals to the courts, will have to adapt to the special needs of stepfamilies. The way things are set up now, stepfamilies have to contend with small—and large—indignities. Most school activities, for example, are structured
35 around intact families. Parents are often allowed only two tickets for special events, like graduation. Although they may be full-time parents

to their spouses' kids, stepparents, in many cases, have no legal rights. If, for example, a child needs emergency surgery, hospitals almost always require the consent of a biological parent or legal guardian. "That's
40 a big issue in the law right now," says Furstenberg. "You bring up a child for 14 years, and yet you have no legal standing, while someone who has never lived with the child does have legal standing. Does that make any sense?"

At least half of children living in stepfamilies are likely to face an
45 additional trauma—the birth of a half-sibling to their parent and the new spouse. This new addition, often intended by the parents as a way to bring the new family together, can have the opposite effect. The older kids often "feel they've been cast in an outsider role," says Nicholas Zill, a Washington D.C. researcher who has studied remarried families.
50 What's even more disturbing is that the new family may not last. Sixty percent of all second marriages are expected to end in divorce, sending everybody—parents and children—into a new emotional maelstrom.

Of course, not all stepchildren are troubled. Some studies have indicated that youngsters who come from families with higher incomes and
55 educational levels do better. The child's age at the time of the parent's remarriage may also be a factor. The Univerity of Virginia's E. Mavis Heterington has found that younger kids and older teenagers are most likely to accept a stepparent. Youngsters in early adolescence, roughly ages 9–15, do the poorest.
60 The attitude of the outside world makes a difference as well. Just a few years ago, people in stepfamilies used to complain that they were the deliberately hidden pages in the American family album. If they were noticed, it was almost always in a negative connotation. Fairy tales hundreds of years old featuring wicked stepmothers set the tone.
65 When Patricia, a New York artist, was growing up in the 1950s, her biggest secret was that her "mother" was not really her mother (who died when she was 3), but her stepmother. She remembers that her stepmother would always wink conspiratorially at her when someone would comment on how much mother and daughter resembled each other.
70 With Patricia's son Michael, the situation was completely different. In the years between Patricia's childhood and her son's, the divorce rate doubled. Multiple marriages are no longer unusual. Patricia was divorced from Michael's father when the boy was only 2. Michael is now 18 and hasn't seen his father since he was 12. Thirteen years ago
75 Patricia married her current husband, Jack. Despite some very rough times, Patricia says Michael never suffered the same stigma she did. "He knows so many other families with various configurations," she says. "He doesn't feel odd."

Even people who aren't in remarried families will have to think
80 about some of these issues as stepfamilies become more and more
prominent. Nontraditional family forms may force us to change our ex-
pectations of the role of the family. "The complexity of families has
reached astounding proportions," says Furstenberg. "It has become
difficult to reckon who is kin, in many respects." In a recent national
85 survey of stepchildren, he found that nearly a quarter did not include
their stepsiblings as part of their family even though they were living
with them.

One of the big questions for the 21st century, says Furstenberg, is
"whether the people we count as kin can be counted on." Will, for ex-
90 ample, stepchildren care for stepparents when they get old? Many experts think that the current generation of stepchildren will rewrite the
rules of family life as they grow up. And they'll be looking for role
models in families who have made it. Patricia, the New York artist, says
that it took a long time, but she feels that Michael considers Jack a real
95 parent. In fact, she had proof when she looked at the quotations next to
her son's picture in his high-school yearbook when he graduated this
spring. "There it was," she recalls, "in between the quotes from Emerson and Led Zeppelin: 'Thanks Mom and Jack. Thanks for everything.'"

Excerpted from Barbara Kantrowitz and Pat Wingert, "Step by Step," *Newsweek*, Special
Issue, 1989.

Check Your Comprehension

1. Why don't we know how many children are currently living in step-
    families?

2. What are some of the examples of discrimination against members
    of stepfamilies?

3. How have attitudes toward stepfamilies changed in the last 50
    years?

Vocabulary: Greek Roots

Look at the list of Greek word parts and their meanings below. Then create ten words by combining a stem or stems with one of the two endings. Write the definition of the word beside it. At least one of your words should contain *two* stems plus an ending.

STEMS:

demo-	*people*	anthropo-	*human*
auto-	*self*	genea-	*race, birth*
bio-	*life*	tele-	*far*
psycho-	*mind*	socio-	*society*

ENDINGS:

-graph(y)   *write*   -logy   *study of*

WORD	DEFINITION
1. _____	_____
2. _____	_____
3. _____	_____
4. _____	_____
5. _____	_____
6. _____	_____
7. _____	_____
8. _____	_____
9. _____	_____
10. _____	_____

Think About It

1. How do you think divorce affects families? Do you know of any examples?

2. The reading states that half of the marriages that started in the 1970s and 1980s will probably end in divorce. Are you surprised by that number? Is it higher or lower than the divorce rate in your own country?

3. Step-relationships complicate family trees. In-laws often do the same. How are in-laws regarded in your culture? (For example, are "mother-in-law jokes" popular?)

4. Below is a diagram showing the relationships and names for members of the family.

English Language Kinship Terminology Chart

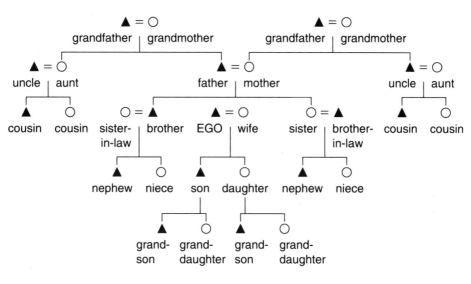

Symbols: Ego = individual (yourself)
○ = female
▲ = male
Attached lines = blood relations
Double lines = relations by marriage
Levels = different generations

(i) Refer to the chart and answer the following questions:
   a. What does Ego call the mother's brother?
   b. What does Ego call the father's brother?
   c. What does Ego call the man whom Ego's sister marries?
   d. Which term is the same for both men and women relatives?
   e. What does Ego call the male children of Ego's sister?
   f. What does Ego call the female children of Ego's sister?
   g. Are the same terms used for the maternal and paternal sides of Ego's family? What about in your own culture?
(ii) Create your own family tree, going back to your grandparents, or farther, if possible.
(iii) Design a family tree that could accommodate the following additional family members:
   a. Ego's paternal grandfather's second wife, who has two daughters, one of whom has a son
   b. Ego's brother's second wife, who has a son from her first marriage; the brother and his second wife also have a daughter together.

Before You Read

Table 4.1   Percent of Adults in the United States Who Are Married (by age)

Women	1987	1980	1970	1960
30 to 34	68.2%	72.7%	83.5%	88.7%
35 to 44	71.5	76.2	82.8	87.1
45 to 54	72.4	75.0	77.9	79.9
55 to 64	67.1	67.1	63.7	66.0
65 and older	39.2	38.0	33.7	37.4
Men				
30 to 34	64.7%	80.9%	86.0%	85.7%
35 to 44	74.7	80.9	86.0	88.7
45 to 54	80.5	81.9	84.6	87.8
55 to 64	81.3	82.4	83.0	84.0
65 and older	74.9	75.5	68.4	70.8

Source: Bureau of the Census, *Current Population Reports, P-20, #423* (Washington, D.C., 1988).

The following reading is an excerpt from *The Joy Luck Club,* a popular novel that tells the story of Chinese immigrants to San Francisco. In this passage, one of the characters, Rose Hsu Jordan, reflects on her divorce, and then thinks back to the time when she met her husband.

Glossary

Golden Gate Park   Large public park in San Francisco

pre-med   Undergraduate university student who is preparing to study medicine

About the Author

Amy Tan was born in Oakland, California, in 1952. Her parents immigrated to the United States from China in 1950. She lives in San Francisco with her husband.

The Joy Luck Club

by Amy Tan

Tonight I'm watching my mother sweep under the same kitchen table, something she does every night after dinner. She gently pokes her broom around the table leg propped up by the Bible. I watch her, sweep after sweep, waiting for the right moment to tell her about Ted and me,
5 that we're getting divorced. When I tell her, I know she's going to say, "This cannot be."

And when I say that it is certainly true, that our marriage is over, I know what else she will say: "Then you must save it."

And even though I know it's hopeless—there's absolutely nothing
10 left to save—I'm afraid if I tell her that, she'll still persuade me to try.

I think it's ironic that my mother wants me to fight the divorce. Seventeen years ago she was chagrined when I started dating Ted. My older sisters had dated only Chinese boys from church before getting married.

Ted and I met in a politics of ecology class when he leaned over and
15 offered to pay me two dollars for last week's notes. I refused the money and accepted a cup of coffee instead. This was during my second semester at UC Berkeley, where I had enrolled as a liberal arts major and later changed to fine arts. Ted was in his third year in pre-med, his choice, he told me, ever since he dissected a fetal pig in the sixth grade.

20 I have to admit that what I initially found attractive in Ted were precisely the things that made him different from my brothers and the Chinese boys I had dated: his brashness; the assuredness in which he asked for things and expected to get them; his opinionated manner; his angular face and lanky body; the thickness of his arms; the fact that his
25 parents immigrated from Tarrytown, New York, not Tientsin, China.

My mother must have noticed these same differences after Ted picked me up one evening at my parents' house. When I returned home, my mother was still up, watching television.

"He is American," warned my mother, as if I had been too blind to
30 notice. "A *waigoren.*"

"I'm American too," I said. "And it's not as if I'm going to marry him or something."

Mrs. Jordan also had a few words to say. Ted had casually invited me to a family picnic, the annual clan reunion held by the polo fields in
35 Golden Gate Park. Although we had dated only a few times in the last month—and certainly had never slept together, since both of us lived at home—Ted introduced me to all his relatives as his girlfriend, which, until then, I didn't know I was.

40 Later, when Ted and his father went off to play volleyball with the others, his mother took my hand, and we started walking along the grass, away from the crowd. She squeezed my palm warmly but never seemed to look at me.

"I'm so glad to meet you *finally,*" Mrs. Jordan said. I wanted to tell her I wasn't really Ted's girlfriend, but she went on. "I think it's nice that 45 you and Ted are having such a lot of fun together. So I hope you won't misunderstand what I have to say."

And then she spoke quietly about Ted's future, his need to concentrate on his medical studies, why it would be years before he could even think about marriage. She assured me she had nothing whatsoever 50 against minorities; she and her husband, who owned a chain of office-supply stores, personally knew many fine people who were oriental, Spanish, and even black. But Ted was going to be in one of those professions where he would be judged by a different standard, by patients and other doctors who might not be as understanding as the Jordans were. 55 She said it was so unfortunate the way the rest of the world was, how unpopular the Vietnam War was.

"Mrs. Jordan, I am not Vietnamese," I said softly, even though I was on the verge of shouting. "And I have no intention of marrying your son."

When Ted drove me home that day, I told him I couldn't see him 60 anymore. When he asked me why, I shrugged. When he pressed me, I told him what his mother had said, verbatim, without comment.

"And you're just going to sit there! Let my mother decide what's right?" he shouted, as if I were a co-conspirator who had turned traitor. I was touched that Ted was so upset.

65 "What should we do?" I asked, and I had a pained feeling I thought was the beginning of love.

Source: Excerpted from Amy Tan, *The Joy Luck Club* (New York: Putnam, 1989).

Check Your Comprehension

1. What sort of woman is Rose's mother? Why does she not want her daughter to date Ted?

2. What sort of woman is Ted's mother? Why does she not want her son to date Rose?

3. What was Rose's reaction to what Ted's mother told her? What was Ted's reaction when Rose told him about it?

4. Why do you think Rose fell in love with Ted?

Vocabulary: Verb Phrases

The following verb phrases, some of which are found in the reading, are made of two words that have a special idiomatic meaning when used together. Fill in the blanks in the eight sentences below with these verb phrases. Use each one only once; remember that, in some cases, the verb and the preposition may be separated. You may need to change the verb form as well.

lean over	prop up	pick up	be up
go off	go on	pick on	go over

1. Although it was midnight, my mother _____ watching television.

2. While the family ate dinner, the youngest son _____ and played Nintendo.

3. I don't think your idea will _____ with the boss very well.

4. John had to _____ to get his coat off the floor.

5. The desk was wobbly, so we _____ it

   _____ with a book.

6. Jane was unhappy because she felt her mother always

   _____ her.

7. "I really like you," Joe's mother said. But then she

   _____, "but I don't want you to marry my son."

8. Ted _____ Rose _____ with his new sportscar.

Think About It

1. The character states that her mother initially opposed her dating Ted, but now will oppose her divorcing him. Why do you think she feels this way?

2. There is a saying in English that "opposites attract." What evidence is there for the truth of this saying in this reading?

3. This passage does not explain why Ted and Rose are going to get a divorce. What reasons can you imagine, drawing on the information contained in this reading?

4. Continue this story by writing a dialogue between Rose and her mother. In this dialogue, Rose tells her mother that she is going to divorce Ted.

PART TWO
Friends: A Friend Indeed

Before You Read

> **friend** (frend) *n.* 1. One who is personally well known by
> oneself and for whom one has warm regard or affection;
> intimate. 2. One with whom one is on speaking terms; an
> associate or acquaintance. 3. One who belongs to the same
> nation, party, etc., as oneself; also, one with whom one is
> united in some purpose, cause, etc.
>
> Source: Adapted from *The Funk and Wagnalls Standard College Dictionary* (New
> York: Funk and Wagnalls, 1968).

In this essay, Judith Viorst discusses the different types of friends
she has had and the different roles they have played for her. She also
discusses how her opinions have changed about what friendship means.
Before you read, think about the following questions:

- Do you have different kinds of friends?
- Have you found it difficult to make friends in the United States?

Glossary

Ingmar Bergman   Swedish film director, also popular in the United
States

Camus   French philosopher and writer (1913–1960)

Newark   Industrial city in the state of New Jersey

Lawrence Welk   Musical conductor who had his own television show;
his style of music was very conservative and most popular with
older people.

Yonkers   Small city in New York State (near New York City)

Brooklyn   Section of New York City

About the Author

Judith Viorst is a professional writer and editor. She writes for many
magazines, most notably *Redbook*, and writes children's books as well.

Friends, Good Friends — and Such Good Friends

by Judith Viorst

Women are friends, I once would have said, when they totally love and support and trust each other, and bare to each other the secrets of their souls, and run—no questions asked—to help each other, and tell harsh truths to each other (no, you can't wear that dress unless you lose
5 ten pounds first) when harsh truths must be told.

Women are friends, I once would have said, when they share the same affection for Ingmar Bergman, plus train rides, cats, warm rain, charades, Camus, and hate with equal ardor Newark and Brussels sprouts and Lawrence Welk and camping.

10 In other words, I once would have said that a friend is a friend all the way, but now I believe that's a narrow point of view. For the friendships I have and the friendships I see are conducted at many levels of intensity, serve many different functions, meet different needs and range from those as all-the-way as the friendship of the soul sisters
15 mentioned above to that of the most nonchalant and casual playmates.

Consider these varieties of friendship:

1. Convenience friends. These are the women with whom, if our paths weren't crossing all the time, we'd have no particular reason to be friends: a next-door neighbor, a woman in our car pool, the mother of
20 one of our children's closest friends or maybe some mommy with whom we serve juice and cookies each week at the Glenwood Co-op Nursery.

Convenience friends are convenient indeed. They'll lend us their cups and silverware for a party. They'll drive our kids to soccer when we're sick. They'll take us to pick up our car when we need a lift to the
25 garage. They'll even take our cats when we go on vacation. As we will for them.

But we don't, with convenience friends, ever come too close or tell too much; we maintain our public face and emotional distance. "Which means," says Elaine, "that I'll talk about being overweight but not about
30 being depressed. Which means I'll admit being mad but not blind with rage. Which means I might say that we're pinched this month but never that I'm worried sick over money."

But which doesn't mean that there isn't sufficient value to be found in these friendships of mutual aid, in convenience friends.

35 2. Special-interest friends. These friendships aren't intimate, and they needn't involve kids or silverware or cats. Their value lies in some interest jointly shared. And so we may have an office friend or a yoga friend or a tennis friend or a friend from the Women's Democratic Club.

"I've got one woman friend," says Joyce, "who likes, as I do, to take
40 psychology courses. Which makes it nice for me—and nice for her. It's
fun to go with someone you know and it's fun to discuss what you've
learned, driving back from classes." And for the most part, she says,
that's all they discuss.

"I'd say that what we're doing is *doing* together, not being to-
45 gether," Suzanne says of her Tuesday-doubles friends. "It's mainly a
tennis relationship, but we play together well. And I guess we all need
to have a couple of playmates."

I agree.

My playmate is a shopping friend, a woman of marvelous taste, a
50 woman who knows exactly *where* to buy *what*, and furthermore is a
woman who always knows beyond a doubt what one ought to be buying. I don't have the time to keep up with what's new in eyeshadow,
hemlines and shoes and whether the smock look is in or finished already. But since (oh, shame!) I care a lot about eyeshadow, hemlines
55 and shoes, and since I don't *want* to wear smocks if the smock look is
finished, I'm very glad to have a shopping friend.

3. Historical friends. We all have a friend who knew us when . . .
maybe way back in Miss Meltzer's second grade, when our family lived
in that three-room flat in Brooklyn, when our dad was out of work for
60 seven months, when our brother Allie got in that fight where they had to
call the police, when our sister married the endodontist from Yonkers
and when, the morning after we lost our virginity, she was the first, the
only, friend we told.

The years have gone by and we've gone separate ways and we've
65 little in common now, but we're still an intimate part of each other's
past. And so whenever we go to Detroit we always go to visit this friend
of our girlhood. Who knows how we looked before our teeth were
straightened. Who knows how we talked before our voice got un-
Brooklyned. Who knows what we ate before we learned about arti-
70 chokes. And who, by her presence, puts us in touch with an earlier part
of ourself, a part of ourself it's important never to lose.

"What this friend means to me and what I mean to her," says Grace,
"is having a sister without sibling rivalry. We know the texture of each
other's lives. She remembers my grandmother's cabbage soup. I remem-
75 ber the way her uncle played the piano. There's simply no other friend
who remembers those things."

4. Crossroads friends. Like historical friends, our crossroads friends
are important for *what was*—for the friendship we shared at a crucial,
now past, time of life. A time, perhaps, when we roomed in college to-
80 gether; or worked as eager young singles in the Big City together; or
went together, as my friend Elizabeth and I did, through pregnancy,
birth and that scary first year of new motherhood.

Crossroads friends forge powerful links, links strong enough to endure with not much more contact than once-a-year letters at Christmas.
85 And out of respect for those crossroads years, for those dramas and dreams we once shared, we will always be friends.

5. Cross-generational friends. Historical friends and crossroads friends seem to maintain a special kind of intimacy—dormant but always ready to be revived—and though we may rarely meet, whenever
90 we do connect, it's personal and intense. Another kind of intimacy exists in the friendships that form across generations in what one woman calls her daughter-mother and her mother-daughter relationships.

Evelyn's friend is her mother's age—"but I share so much more than I ever could with my mother"—a woman she talks to of music, of
95 books and of life. "What I get from her is the benefit of her experience. What she gets—and enjoys—from me is a youthful perspective. It's a pleasure for both of us."

I have in my own life a precious friend, a woman of 65 who has lived very hard, who is wise, who listens well; who has been where I am and
100 can help me understand it; and who represents not only an ultimate ideal mother to me but also the person I'd like to be when I grow up.

In our daughter role we tend to do more than our share of self-revelation; in our mother role we tend to receive what's revealed. It's another kind of pleasure—playing wise mother to a questing younger
105 person. It's another very lovely kind of friendship.

6. Part-of-a-couple friendships. Some of the women we call our friends we never see alone—we see them as part of a couple at couples' parties. And though we share interests in many things and respect each other's views, we aren't moved to deepen the relationship. Whatever the
110 reason, a lack of time or—and this is more likely—a lack of chemistry, our friendship remains in the context of a group. But the fact that our feeling on seeing each other is always, "I'm *so* glad she's here" and the fact that we spend half the evening talking together says that this too, in its own way, counts as a friendship.

115 (Other part-of-a-couple friends are the friends that came with the marriage, and some of these are friends we could live without. But sometimes, alas, she married our husband's best friend; and sometimes, alas, she *is* our husband's best friend. And so we find ourselves dealing with her, somewhat against our will, in a spirit of what I'll call *reluctant*
120 friendship.)

7. Men who are friends. I wanted to write just of women friends, but the women I've talked to won't let me—they say I must mention man-woman friendships too. For these friendships can be just as close and as dear as those that we form with women. Listen to Lucy's description
125 of one such friendship:

"We've found we have things to talk about that are different from what he talks about with my husband and different from what I talk about with his wife. So sometimes we call on the phone or meet for lunch. There are similar intellectual interests—we always pass on to 130   each other the book that we love—but there's also something tender and caring too."

In a couple of crises, Lucy says, "He offered himself for talking and helping. And when someone died in his family he wanted me there. The sexual, flirty part of our friendship is very small—but *some*—just 135   enough to make it fun and different." She thinks—and I agree—that the sexual part, though small, is always *some*, is always there when a man and a woman are friends.

It's only in the past few years that I've made friends with men, in the sense of a friendship that's *mine*, not just part of two couples. And 140   achieving with them the ease and the trust I've found with women friends has value indeed. Under the dryer at home last week, putting on mascara and rouge, I comfortably sat and talked with a fellow named Peter. Peter, I finally decided, could handle the shock of me minus mascara under the dryer. Because we care for each other. Because we're 145   friends.

There are medium friends, and pretty good friends, and very good friends indeed, and these friendships are defined by their level of intimacy. And what we'll reveal at each of these levels of intimacy is calibrated with care. We might tell a medium friend, for example, that yes- 150   terday we had a fight with our husband. And we might tell a pretty good friend that this fight with our husband made us so mad that we slept on the couch. And we might tell a very good friend that the reason we got so mad in that fight that we slept on the couch had something to do with that girl who works in his office. But it's only to our very best friends 155   that we're willing to tell all, to tell what's going on with that girl in his office.

The best of friends, I still believe, totally love and support and trust each other, and bare to each other the secrets of their souls, and run— no questions asked—to help each other, and tell harsh truths to each 160   other when they must be told.

But we needn't agree about everything (only 12-year-old girl friends agree about *everything*) to tolerate each other's point of view. To accept without judgment. To give and to take without ever keeping score. And to *be* there, as I am for them and as they are for me, to comfort our 165   sorrows, to celebrate our joys.

From Judith Viorst, "Friends, Good Friends—and Such Good Friends," *Redbook*, October 1977.

Check Your Comprehension

1. What is the value the author finds in "convenience" friends?
2. What is the value of "historical" friends?
3. How has Viorst's opinion of what it means to be a friend changed?

Vocabulary: Using New Vocabulary

Create twelve sentences, using one of the following words in each.

ardor	nonchalant	charades	smock
hemline	sibling	dormant	crucial
revelation	quest	forge	artichoke

1. _____
2. _____
3. _____
4. _____
5. _____
6. _____
7. _____
8. _____
9. _____
10. _____
11. _____
12. _____

Think About It

1. The preceding article appeared in a women's magazine, mainly for women. If it had been written for men, would the categories have been different? Which ones might have been different?

2. What is the difference between acquaintances and friends? Do you agree that all the author's categories illustrate types of friends, or are some of them just acquaintances?

3. The author says she doesn't think it is necessary for friends always to agree. What *must* you agree on if you are to be close friends (for example, politics, religious beliefs, moral values)?

4. Have you found Americans' definition of who is a friend different from that in your own culture? If so, is it a broader or narrower definition? Is one preferable to the other, in your opinion?

5. At the beginning of this section, there is a dictionary definition of "friend." Without referring to it, write your own definition.

6. Is there a difference between men's and women's friendships in your culture? Are women and men generally friends with each other in your culture?

7. Write your own categories of friendship. Think of a name and a brief definition for each. After you complete your list, work with a partner or a small group and compare your lists. Did your lists have any descriptions in common? On which points did you differ?

Before You Read

Table 4.2   Population Density of Selected Countries of the World

Country	Population/ Sq. Mile	Country	Population/ Sq. Mile
U.S.S.R.	34	Hungary	294
U.S.	69	P.R.C. (China)	301
Colombia	74	Poland	318
Iran	87	Dominican Republic	399
Cambodia	100	Italy	496
Iraq	112	Vietnam	538
Mexico	114	Israel	556
Egypt	145	Philippines	575
Syria	174	India	670
Turkey	188	El Salvador	698
Greece	198	Lebanon	848
Cuba	239	Japan	861
Indonesia	244	South Korea	1155
France	266	R.O.C. (Taiwan)	1642
		Singapore	11309

Source: Bureau of the Census, *Statistical Abstract of the United States, 1989* (Washington, D.C., 1989), table 1403.

In this second passage by Andy Rooney, he discusses the relationships Americans have with their neighbors. He also talks about the "typical" American neighborhood.

Before you read, think about the following questions:

- Do you know your neighbors?

- What type of relationship do you think you should have with your neighbors?

About the Author

Andy Rooney began his writing career as a correspondent for *The Stars and Stripes*, a military newspaper, during World War II. He has since written for television and many newspapers. He is currently well known for his short, humorous weekly contribution to the television news program *Sixty Minutes*, which is broadcast on Sunday nights.

Love Thy Neighbor
by Andy Rooney

It seems to me that neighbors are going out of style in America. The friend next door from whom you borrowed four eggs or a ladder has moved, and the people in there now are strangers.

Some of the old folklore of neighborliness is impractical or silly, 5 and it may be just as well that our relations with our neighbors are changing. The biblical commandment to "Love Thy Neighbor" was probably a poor translation of what must have originally been "Respect Thy Neighbor." Love can't be called up on order.

Fewer than half the people in the United States live in the same 10 house they lived in five years ago, so there's no reason to love the people who live next door to you just because they happened to wander into a real estate office that listed the place next door to yours. The only thing neighbors have in common to begin with is proximity, and unless something more develops, that isn't reason enough to be best friends. It 15 sometimes happens naturally, but the chances are very small that your neighbors will be your choice as buddies. Or that you will be theirs, either.

The best relationship with neighbors is one of friendly distance. You say hello, you small-talk if you see them in the yard, you discuss 20 problems as they arise and you help each other in an emergency. It's the kind of arrangement where you see more of them in the summer than in the winter. The driveway or the hedge or the fence between you is not really a cold shoulder, but it is a clear boundary. We all like clearly defined boundaries for ourselves.

25 If neighbors have changed, neighborhoods have not. They still comprise the same elements. If you live in a real neighborhood you can be sure most of the following people will be found there:

—One family with more kids than they can take care of.

—A dog that gets into garbage cans.

30 —One grand home with a family so rich that they really aren't part of the neighborhood.

—A bad kid who steals or sets fire to things, although no one has ever been able to prove it.

—People who leave their Christmas decorations up until March.

35 —A grouchy woman who won't let the kids cut through her backyard.

—Someone who doesn't cut their grass more than twice a summer.

—Someone who cuts their grass twice a week and one of the times always seems to be Sunday morning at 7:30.

40 —One driveway with a junky-looking pickup truck or trailer that's always sitting there.

—A family that never seems to turn off any lights in the house.

—A teenager who plays the radio too loud in the summer with the windows open.

—Someone who leaves their barking dog out until 11:30 most nights.

45 —One mystery couple. They come and go but hardly anyone ever sees them and no one knows what they do.

—A couple that has loud parties all the time with guests that take an hour to leave once they get outside and start shouting good-bye at each other.

50 —Someone who doesn't pull the shades.

—A house with a big maple tree whose owners don't rake the leaves until most of them have blown into someone else's yard.

It is easier to produce nostalgia about a neighborhood than about a community, but a community is probably a better unit. A neighborhood
55 is just a bunch of individuals who live in proximity, but a community is a group of people who rise above their individual limitations to get some things done in town.

From Andy Rooney, *And More by Andy Rooney*, 1983.

Check Your Comprehension

1. Why does the author think it is "just as well" that our relationships with our neighbors may be changing?

2. What does the author think is the "best" relationship to have with your neighbors?

3. What is the difference between a community and a neighborhood? Under what circumstances can they be the same?

Vocabulary: Crosswords

Below is a crossword puzzle. Read the definitions and then write the word that fits each definition in the series of blanks, the first of which contains the number corresponding to the definition. All the words to be used can be found in the reading.

ACROSS

1. A type of wall creating a boundary between two pieces of land

5. A group of people living together who may share interests or beliefs

6. A piece of land found behind a house, usually covered with grass

7. Nearness to; in _____ to

8. A row of bushes or trees that serves as a border or boundary

9. Light conversation about unimportant subjects (hyphenated word)

10. A tree whose leaves turn color and fall in the autumn

DOWN

2. Fondness for things in the past

3. The knowledge and habits from an earlier time, still in use by a group of people

4. Bad-tempered

6. Friends, pals (informal)

7. A type of small truck

Think About It

1. How are U.S. neighborhood relationships different from those in your own country?

2. What is your current neighborhood like? Does it have any of the "characters" that are described in this reading? Are you one of those neighborhood types?

3. What community or communities do you belong to currently? (For example, you may be a member of a university or college community.)

4. Write a description of the most important community you belong to, either here or in your home town. What function does that community serve? What benefits do its members derive from it? What shortcomings or limitations does it have?

Synthesis

Discussion and Debate

1. In what ways do you think people treat their families differently from their friends and neighbors? In which ways do they treat their families better? Are there any ways in which they treat them worse?

2. "Blood is thicker than water" is a popular proverb among English speakers. What do you think it means? Is there a similar proverb in your first language? Explain it to your classmates.

3. It is often said that Americans are very informal in their relationships with other people. Do you agree? What evidence do you find for this in relationships with both family and friends?

4. Adoption—the legal acceptance of a stranger's child as part of your own family—is a popular practice in the United States. How is adoption viewed in your own culture? What is your opinion of this practice?

5. Ask your classmates another question about the material covered in this chapter.

Writing Topics

1. Write a paragraph explaining the difference between "friendship" and "kinship."

2. Write a short biography of a friend or relative whose life has been very interesting. Explain the relationship of this person to you, or how you met him or her.

3. Write an essay in which you explain the difference between the levels of formality shown between friends and family in your own culture. How does this compare to what you know about American culture?

On Your Own

1. On your own, or with a friend, visit a neighborhood that's different from your own. What was it like? What makes it different? Describe this neighborhood to your classmates.

2. Interview an American friend or acquaintance about the topics included in this chapter. Some of the questions you may want to ask are:

    a. How many brothers and sisters do you have?
    b. What are your parents like?
    c. Do you have any step- or half-brothers and sisters?
    d. Do you remember your first best friend?
    e. Who are your neighbors?

    Tape record the interview or take detailed notes. Then write a short report on your interviewee. Did his or her responses surprise you in any way? Were they different from what you expected after you had read this chapter?

3. Many popular television programs feature family life. Check your local television listings, and watch two different shows that feature families—one from an earlier time and one from the present time. (Older shows include "Leave It To Beaver," "Father Knows Best," "The Donna Reed Show," "All In the Family," and "The Jeffersons." More recent shows include "The Cosby Show," "Who's the Boss?," "Family Ties," "Wonder Years," "Roseanne," or "Growing Pains.")

    Answer the following questions about the shows you have seen:

    a. What was the main problem in each of the shows you watched?
    b. How are the characters different in the two programs?
    c. What things are "outdated" about the older show you watched?
    d. Which program did you prefer? Why?

The American Landscape

PART ONE
Regions: States of Mind

Before You Read

Table 5.1   States of the United States and Their Populations, 1988

California	28,168,000	Oklahoma	3,263,000
New York	17,898,000	Connecticut	3,241,000
Texas	16,780,000	Iowa	2,834,000
Florida	12,377,000	Oregon	2,741,000
Pennsylvania	12,027,000	Mississippi	2,627,000
Illinois	11,544,000	Kansas	2,487,000
Ohio	10,872,000	Arkansas	2,422,000
Michigan	9,300,000	West Virginia	1,884,000
New Jersey	7,720,000	Utah	1,691,000
North Carolina	6,526,000	Nebraska	1,601,000
Georgia	6,401,000	New Mexico	1,510,000
Virginia	5,996,000	Maine	1,206,000
Massachusetts	5,871,000	New Hampshire	1,097,000
Indiana	5,575,000	Hawaii	1,093,000
Missouri	5,139,000	Nevada	1,060,000
Tennessee	4,919,000	Idaho	999,000
Wisconsin	4,858,000	Rhode Island	995,000
Maryland	4,644,000	Montana	804,000
Washington	4,619,000	South Dakota	715,000
Louisiana	4,420,000	North Dakota	663,000
Minnesota	4,306,000	Delaware	660,000
Alabama	4,127,000	District of Columbia	620,000
Kentucky	3,721,000	Vermont	556,000
South Carolina	3,493,000	Alaska	513,000
Arizona	3,466,000	Wyoming	471,000
Colorado	3,290,000		

Source: Bureau of the Census, *Statistical Abstract of the United States, 1989* (Washington, D.C., 1989).

The following excerpts examine the people and attitudes in the two largest states of the United States: Texas and Alaska. They are written from the point of view of an "outside observer"—that is, an Englishman visiting the United States.

Before you read, think about the following questions:

• What image do you have of Texas? Where did you get that image?

• What do you know about Alaska?

Glossary

Yankees   People from the northern and western states that were
not part of the Confederacy during the American Civil War
(1861–1865)

Edna Ferber   Popular twentieth-century author who received the
Pulitzer prize

About the Author

Trevor Fishlock is a New York correspondent for the London *Times.*

The State of America
by Trevor Fishlock

Texas: Boss of the Plains

Texans have bursting pride and love attention. They also have a
thick streak of shortsighted greed and, even by American standards, a
noted disposition to violence. When they hear this sort of criticism they
5 usually ascribe it to the ignorance and jealousy of stuffy Yankees who
have not spent enough time in the state to understand it. For such
avowedly robust people they are surprisingly sensitive. They hated
Edna Ferber's novel *Giant*, which scourged Texan vulgarity, racism
and the *mores* of millionaires, but they bought it in great quantities and
10 packed cinemas to see the film. They would rather be talked about than
not, and if you do not talk about them they do it for you.

In claiming special qualities for themselves, Texans have had to become reconciled to the fact that a large number of them are not native.
In the last century "Gone to Texas" was a commonplace graffito daubed
15 on barns in other states, and in recent years "Gone to Texas" has, figu-
ratively, been written on the front doors of millions of Americans and
also Mexicans. In the early 1980s newcomers accounted for nearly two-
thirds of the state's population increase. But Texans do not believe they
are being diluted. They maintain that Texanhood, or Texianism, is a
20 matter of attitude and that Texanic qualities exist in abundance in many
Americans, regardless of their birthplace: it is when these people are
planted in Texas, and nourished by its atmosphere, that they flower like
true Texans. A man may not be born in Texas, which is unfortunate; but
he can be born to be Texan.

25   *The Inside: Alaska*

Many Alaskans are urban, young and raising families, here for a while, and trying to make money before moving to somewhere warmer. But many are staying. While most remain in Anchorage and other centers, some set out to build a cabin in the wilderness and live by hunting,
30   trapping and fishing, learning how to skin a muskrat and moose, how to survive terrible weather, how to be truly in tune with the land, taking pleasure in great silence and unpeopled immensity. To settle the frontier the state has a homesteading program, based on the federal Homestead Act of 1864, which was a key event in the opening up of the
35   American west. Hundreds of Alaskans are awarded parcels of wilderness land in an annual lottery and undertake to invest sweat equity, to build a home within three years and clear and cultivate the land within five. Alaskans love reading about Alaska, and two of the most popular books are a manual on log cabin building and a collection of tales about
40   grizzly bears, of which Alaska is a stronghold. Log cabin life is for the stout-hearted few with the springs of adventure strong in them, and these wilderness Alaskans are remarkable. Some are refugees of one kind or another. Several hundred are Vietnam veterans, tortured by their experiences of war and unable to fit into normal urban life, seek-
45   ing solace in the wilds.

There are few roads in the bush. It is hard to build them on permafrost—permanently frozen ground—because it is unstable. There is a 470-mile railway link between Anchorage and Fairbanks, and people in the hamlets along the way can flag down the train when they want to
50   get on. Otherwise the only practical way of reaching most of the great land is by aircraft. Nowhere else in the world is there such a high concentration of private aircraft in relation to the population. There is one plane for every seventy-five Alaskans, and one person in every forty-five is a qualified pilot. People here are as familiar with aircraft as they
55   are with cars, and flying lore and epic take-offs and landings are favorite subjects of Alaskan conversation. Thousands depend on the pilots of small planes to deliver their groceries, heating oil, mail and medicines, and to fly them to a doctor, to the nearest town, or to a reunion dinner. This is, above all, bush pilot country, and the exploits of pilots,
60   many of them colorful and daring men, the modern explorers of Alaska, are the stuff of legends. Alaska is an outpost of "real flying" where seat-of-the-pants pilots set down planes on rough airstrips, beaches, frozen marshes, glaciers and lakes, often in poor weather. The weather is often foul and unpredictable and planes ice up and pilots get lost. News-
65   papers here publish warnings about the dangers of drinking and flying.

From Trevor Fishlock, *The State of America* (London: Faber & Faber, 1986).

Check Your Comprehension

1. Why did Texans hate the book *Giant* and the film made of it? Why did so many Texans read the book or see the film?
2. What qualifies someone as a Texan, according to the author?
3. According to Fishlock, what type of people are Alaskans?
4. Why are there so many planes in Alaska?

Vocabulary: Paraphrasing

Rewrite each of the following sentences, paraphrasing the words that are italicized (excluding, of course, the title of Ferber's novel; you may reword the rest of the sentence if necessary).

1. They hated Edna Ferber's novel *Giant*, which *scourged* Texan *vulgarity*, racism and the *mores* of millionaires.

    _____

    _____

2. In the last century "Gone to Texas" was a *commonplace graffito daubed on* barns in other states.

    _____

    _____

3. It is when these people are *planted* in Texas, and *nourished* by its *atmosphere* that they *flower* like true Texans.

    _____

    _____

4. Many Alaskans *take pleasure in* great silence and *unpeopled immensity.*

    _____

    _____

5. Two of the most popular books are a *manual on log cabin building* and a collection of tales about grizzly bears, of which Alaska is a *stronghold.*

    _____

    _____

6. Log cabin life is for the *stout-hearted few* with the *springs of adventure* strong in them.

    _____

    _____

7. People in the *hamlets* along the way can *flag down* the train when they want to get on.

   _____

   _____

8. Alaska is an *outpost* of "real flying" where *seat-of-the-pants* pilots set down planes on rough airstrips.

   _____

   _____

Think About It

1. According to the information given in this reading and your own knowledge, how are Alaskans and Texans different? Are there are ways in which they are the same?

2. Would you prefer to live in Texas or in Alaska? Why?

3. Are there areas of the country where the people have a distinctive regional "character"? Explain.

4. Read the following facts about Alaska and Texas. Then write seven sentences comparing the two states in regard to the point indicated.

	ALASKA	TEXAS
Became a state of the U.S.	1959	1845
1987 population	525,000	16,789,000
Size (square miles)	570,833	262,017
Population of largest city	248,263 (Anchorage)	1,595,138 (Houston)
Number of people who moved into the state in 1984	970	42,180
Percent of the population less than 15 years old	28	25
Number of serious crimes for every 1000 people	59	66

Source: *Information Please Almanac, 1989.*

1. (area) _____

2. (age) _____

3. (city) _____

4. (crime) _____

5. (children) _____

6. (population) _____

7. (new inhabitants) _____

Before You Read

Figure 5.1   Population of the United States by Region in 1950 and 1987

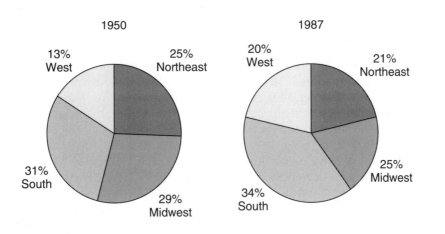

Source: Bureau of the Census, *Statistical Abstract of the United States, 1989* (Washington, D.C., 1989), tables 22 and 30.

The following reading concerns our most populous state, California. The author discusses the idea of a Californian identity and personality. He also discusses some of the problems facing the state.

Before you read, think about the following questions:

• What is your impression of California (whether you have been there or not)?

• What do you think "Californians" are like?

Glossary

Manhattan Island   Island on which part of New York City (Manhattan) is located

mesoamerican people   Central Americans (*meso-* means *middle*)

spur track/main line   Railroad terms; a main line is a major railroad route; a spur track is a smaller route that connects to the main line.

About the Author

Wallace Stegner is an award winning writer; he has won the O. Henry Award for his short stories, the National Book Award, and the Pulitzer Prize. He is also the former editor of the magazine *American West.*

California Rising

by Wallace Stegner

One out of every ten Americans is a Californian. There are many more Californians in the world than there are Australians and New Zealanders combined, more Californians than all the Norwegians, Swedes, Danes, Finns, and Icelanders in Scandinavia, more than twice as many
5 Californians as Hungarians, Portuguese or Greeks. Nations that have shaken the world, and some that still trouble it, look puny by comparison with this single state. The California economy exceeds that of all but a handful of nations. The state has a fantastic variety of topographies, climates, products, natural beauties. It has the biggest con-
10 gressional delegation, and it has produced—though not everyone brags about this—two out of the last four presidents, and become the adopted home of a third.

Ask a Hungarian, a Norwegian, or a Greek who he is, and he can tell you, probably with pride. He is bonded to his fellow countrymen by
15 blood, language, history, folkways, evolved arts, shared triumphs and shared defeats, even by the degree of inbreeding and adaptation that produces a recognizable physical type. And he is definable to others as to himself; outsiders have an image of him that may be wrong in detail but is broadly accurate.

20 But ask a Californian who he is and you may get any of two dozen answers, in two dozen languages. Native sons and daughters will identify themselves as Californians without hesitation—indeed, with the same sort of patriotic pride that a Greek or Norwegian might show. But immigrants, and we are many, may not. I tried it on the luncheon table
25 the other day and found that the people seated at it, though they have all lived in California since at least the 1940s, still think of themselves as Iowans, Kansans, or Scotsmen. Identification with place, they agreed, has much to do with growing up in it, and may not be fully achieved short of a couple of generations. But they agreed on something else,
30 too: non-Californians though they were, they didn't want to live anywhere else, including the places where they grew up.

A generation ago, writing on this same subject, I concluded that California was "America only more so . . . the national culture at its most energetic end. . . . In a prosperous country we are more pros-
35 perous than most; in an urban country more urban than most; in a gadget-happy country more addicted to gadgets; in a mobile country more mobile; in a tasteless country more tasteless; in a creative country more energetically creative; in an optimistic society more optimistic, in an anxious society more anxious."

40   It did not seem to me then that California could be called a cultural region. It didn't have the isolation, the homogeneity, or the humility to be called a region. It didn't feel like any spur track, it felt like a main line, and it was likely to assert that if Columbus had landed on the West Coast instead of the West Indies, Manhattan Island would still belong to
45   the Indians.

That was in 1959, at the height of the postwar boom. With the aid of hindsight I would not really change that judgment, but I would temper it. For it seems clear now that in 1959, and before it, and after it, California has not only been America only more so, it has sometimes been
50   America in the worst sense of the word. It has plundered itself, it has permitted the wide excesses of wide-open opportunism and uncontrollable growth. Mainly over water, it has split itself politically in two.

Now things have changed and grown tighter. We are making real estate millionaires in smaller numbers. We are tearing down and selling
55   off the schools that for a while we were completing at the rate of two or three a week. We live at a different point on the population curve than during those years when more than 50 percent of the population was under 25. We have seen the influx of millions of immigrants, many of whom will not make it to full citizenship for two or three generations, if
60   ever. The movement of Pacific and mesoamerican peoples into the state has postponed for a long time the development of a recognizable California type—either that, or it has guaranteed the continuation and widening of the gap between haves and have-nots that has ominous economic and racial possibilities for the future.

Excerpted from Wallace Stegner, "California Rising," *New West*, October 1981.

Check Your Comprehension

1. How does the author think a Californian identity is different from any other national identity?

2. Why doesn't the author consider California a "cultural region"?

3. What does the author mean when he says California is sometimes "America in the worst sense of the word"?

4. What are some of the problems facing California?

Vocabulary: Country Names

Fill in the following table with the correct forms for either the names of the country, its inhabitants, or the main language spoken there. The first one is done for you.

COUNTRY	INHABITANTS	LANGUAGE
1. Australia	*Australians*	*English*
2. _____	Brazilians	_____
3. _____	Danes	_____
4. France	_____	_____
5. Germany	_____	_____
6. _____	_____	Greek
7. Hungary	_____	_____
8. Italy	_____	_____
9. _____	_____	Japanese
10. South Korea	_____	_____
11. _____	Mexicans	_____
12. Norway	_____	_____
13. People's Republic of China	_____	_____
14. _____	Portuguese	_____
15. Republic of China (Taiwan)	_____	_____
16. Scotland	_____	_____
17. _____	Spaniards	_____
18. Sweden	_____	_____
19. The United States of America	_____	_____
20. _____	Austrians	_____

Think About It

1. Reread the fourth paragraph of this selection. Can you think of any examples to support the following ideas from Stegner's argument?

    *   California's "tastelessness"
    *   California's "creativity"
    *   California's "mobility"

2. The author speaks of the "widening of the gap between the haves and have-nots." What does he mean by this? What evidence is there for this in the United States? Is it happening in your culture or in other cultures you know about?

3. Why do you think California has become the most populous and influential state in the United States?

4. Alone or with a partner, choose a popular tourist attraction in California. Make a list of all the reasons that someone should visit there. Then prepare an oral argument to convince people that they should visit that particular attraction. You may choose from the list below or a tourist attraction not in the list.

    a. Sea World
    b. San Francisco's Chinatown
    c. Yosemite
    d. Death Valley
    e. San Diego Zoo
    f. San Francisco's Fisherman's Wharf
    g. Redwood Forest
    h. Palm Springs
    i. Malibu
    j. Monterey Bay Aquarium
    k. Venice Beach
    l. Disneyland
    m. Big Sur

PART TWO
Lifestyles: City Slickers vs. Country Bumpkins

Before You Read

An Immigrant Family in New York

The following reading first discusses Ellis Island, a part of New York City, which was the main point of entry into the United States for millions of immigrants during the nineteenth and early twentieth centuries. It then tells the story of one Italian immigrant who passed through Ellis Island.

Before you read, think about the following questions:

- What are your country's immigration policies?
- What do you think might be the advantages and disadvantages of a "nation of immigrants"?

Glossary

Emma Lazarus   American poet and essayist, born in New York City, 1849, and died in 1887; she is best known as the writer of the poem that is inscribed on the Statue of Liberty.

P.S. 22 in Queens   Public School No. 22 in the Queens Borough (section) of New York City

Prohibition   Period from 1920 to 1933 during which it was illegal to produce or drink any alcoholic beverage in the United States

Ellis Island
by Dinitia Smith

For many Americans, Ellis Island is a holy ground, the entry point for the ancestors of more than 100 million people, 40 percent of the country's population. From 1892 to 1924, more than 12 million people entered the United States through Ellis Island. On one day (April 17,
5   1907) 11,747 immigrants were processed there.
In a nation of well over a hundred ethnic groups, Ellis Island is the setting of America's one great unifying epic. While other countries have their own national legends, France has its Chanson de Roland, Spain its El Cid—America has the myth of the Golden Door, through which the
10 "huddled masses yearning to breathe free," as Emma Lazarus puts it, stepped and found freedom and prosperity at last. Paradoxically, that myth is being rethought and rewritten just as the museum at Ellis Island—started in a burst of patriotic nostalgia—is about to be dedicated.

The image of the immigrant as poor, oppressed, and uprooted is giv-
15 ing way under the weight of new scholarship. Most people who came
to the New World during the peak immigration years had at least the
means to pay for the journey, and the stamina and health to withstand
it. They came seeking better jobs more often than freedom. (Of course,
many didn't find freedom at all. Not only were blacks imported as
20 slaves, but before 1780, 75 percent of all white immigrants who settled
south of New England were indentured servants.) For the most part,
the people who came willingly brought the structures of their old cultures with them and used their traditions to build lives there. Perhaps
most startling of all, it has recently been shown that a third of all those
25 who had come to America during the twentieth century have chosen to
go home again—10 million out of 30 million people.

New York, meanwhile, is once again becoming a city of émigrés.
More and more foreign-born people are settling here. By the year 2000,
56 percent of New York City's population will be immigrants and their
30 children. Dominicans are currently the biggest group, followed by
Jamaicans and Chinese. At P.S. 22 in Queens, the students speak twenty
languages. And in the New York City courts these days, there is a fre-
quent demand for interpreters who know Wolof, a language spoken in
West Africa and in New York by Senegalese street merchants.

35 The new immigrants have reversed the city's declining population
and are stemming the decrease in the labor force. They are revitalizing
dying neighborhoods, setting up shop in empty stores on Flatbush Avenue, bringing the infinite variety of their cultures to the great mix that is
the city.

40   *A New Blueprint*

Even today, Guerino Salerni remembers the touch of his grandfather Luigi's whiskers as he kissed him goodbye. When Salerni, now 84,
talks about leaving for America in 1919—when he was 14—tears still
come to his eyes. "It was the last time I saw him," says Salerni. "He was
45 quite a fellow." Guerino Salerni came from a family of stonemasons in a
medieval hill town in the region of Abruzzi, east of Rome. As a boy, Salerni could build a home of stones in the fields and it would stand.

Salerni's father had first come to the United States in 1896. He
found work in construction, traveling back and forth between the U.S.
50 and Italy regularly, each time begetting a child. In 1918, Salerni's father
decided it was time for the rest of the family to come. Like many immigrants, they traveled with a group from their village. There was Salerni's
stepmother (his mother had died), his sister, and a dozen ladies whose
husbands had already journeyed ahead.

55   Salerni hadn't seen his father in five years, but as the ship docked
near Ellis Island, he spotted him down below in a motorboat. "Where's
Mama? Where's Mama?" his father cried. Salerni's stepmother threw
down a bottle of Centerba, a liqueur from Abruzzi, in greeting—even
though America was in the midst of Prohibition.

60   Because there had been a death from typhoid fever aboard the ship,
Salerni spent ten days in quarantine before he was reunited with his father for good. When he grew up, Salerni became an architect, working
on a number of projects in New York City—including the construction
of East River Drive—continuing the traditions of his Italian ancestors.

From *New York Magazine*, August 27, 1990.

Check Your Comprehension

1. What is meant by the "myth of the Golden Door" (line 9)?
2. According to the author, what were the real circumstances and mo-
   tives of the immigrant in the early part of this century?
3. What benefits does the author see immigrants bringing to New York?

Vocabulary: Using Prepositions

Read the following sentences and insert the correct preposition in the
blanks.

1. _____ many Americans, Ellis Island was the entry point _____ the
   ancestors _____ more than 100 million people.
2. _____ April 17, 1907, 11,747 immigrants were processed _____ Ellis
   Island.
3. Many immigrants came _____ "The Golden Door" and found freedom and prosperity _____ last.
4. Most people who came _____ the New World during the peak immigration years had _____ least the means _____ pay _____ the journey.
5. _____ 1780, 75 percent _____ all white immigrants who settled
   south _____ New England were indentured servants.
6. A third _____ all those who had come _____ America chose _____
   go home again—10 million _____ _____ 30 million people.

7. _____ the year 2000, 56 percent of New York City's population will be immigrants and their children.

8. Dominicans are currently the biggest group, followed _____ Jamaicans and Chinese.

9. The new immigrants are slowing the decrease _____ the labor force.

10. They are setting _____ shop in empty stores _____ Flatbush Avenue.

Think About It

1. What was your first day in the United States like? How do you think it compared to the experiences of people like Mr. Salerni?

2. The words inscribed on the Statue of Liberty are taken from a poem written in 1883 by Emma Lazarus, part of which is given below:

THE NEW COLOSSUS

Give me your tired, your poor,
Your huddled masses yearning to breathe free,
The wretched refuse of your teeming shore,
Send these, the homeless, tempest-tost, to me,
I lift my lamp beside the golden door!

Look up any words in this poem you don't understand, and rewrite it in everyday language. Then answer the following questions:

a. What is the relationship between this poem and the article above?
b. What do you think about this poem and the ideas expressed by it?

3. Interview a U.S.-born American whose ancestors immigrated through Ellis Island. Ask him or her how much is known about the family's experience. Tape-record the interview or take detailed notes. Write the interview in story form, like the story of Mr. Salerni told in the article above.

Before You Read

Figure 5.2   Number of Inhabitants in the Country or in Cities, 1950–1987

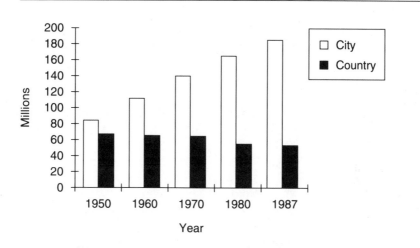

Source: Bureau of the Census, *Statistical Abstract of the United States, 1989* (Washington, D.C., 1989), table 32.

In this humorous reading, the author describes what life was like growing up in a small city in Iowa. He uses hyperbole—that is, extreme exaggeration—to illustrate what life was like there.

Before you read, think about the following questions:

- Are you from a small town or from the city? What was it like growing up there?
- How do city people feel about country people in your culture?

Glossary

Firestone   Tire manufacturing company located in Des Moines, Iowa

Jack Kerouac   Twentieth-century American writer, most famous for a book called *On the Road*

Viewmaster   Device with which you can look at photographic transparencies; it has two eyepieces, so that when you look through it, the image appears to be three-dimensional.

Herbert Hoover   Thirty-first president of the United States, born in Iowa in 1874

John Deere   Name of a manufacturing company that makes tractors and other agricultural machinery

About the Author

Bill Bryson is a writer from Iowa who lives in England. He is the author of the book *The Mother Tongue: English and How It Got That Way.*

Fat Girls in Des Moines

by Bill Bryson

I come from Des Moines. Somebody had to. When you come from Des Moines you either accept the fact without question and settle down with a local girl named Bobbi and get a job at the Firestone factory and live there forever and ever, or you spend your adolescence moaning at
5 length about what a dump it is and how you can't wait to get out, and then you settle down with a local girl named Bobbi and get a job at the Firestone factory and live there forever and ever.

Hardly anyone leaves. This is because Des Moines is the most powerful hypnotic known to man. Outside town there is a big sign that
10 says: WELCOME TO DES MOINES. THIS IS WHAT DEATH IS LIKE. There isn't really. I just made that up. But the place does get a grip on you. People who have nothing to do with Des Moines drive in off the interstate, looking for gas or hamburgers, and stay forever. There's a New Jersey couple up the street from my parents' house whom you
15 see wandering around from time to time looking faintly puzzled but strangely serene. Everybody in Des Moines is strangely serene.

When I was growing up I used to think that the best thing about coming from Des Moines was that it meant you didn't come from any-where else in Iowa. By Iowa standards, Des Moines is a Mecca of cos-
20 mopolitanism, a dynamic hub of wealth and education, where people wear three-piece suits and dark socks, often simultaneously. During the annual state high school basketball tournament, when the hayseeds from out in the state would flood into the city for a week, we used to accost them downtown and snidely offer to show them how to ride an
25 escalator or negotiate a revolving door. This wasn't always so far from reality. My friend Stan, when he was about sixteen, had to go and stay with his cousin in some remote, dusty hamlet called Dog Water or Dunceville or some such improbable spot—the kind of place where if a dog gets run over by a truck everybody goes out to have a look at it. By
30 the second week, delirious with boredom, Stan insisted that he and his cousin drive the fifty miles into the county town, Hooterville, and find something to do. They went bowling at an alley with warped lanes and chipped balls and afterwards had a chocolate soda and looked at a *Playboy* in a drugstore, and on the way home the cousin sighed with
35 immense satisfaction and said, "Gee, thanks Stan. That was the best time I ever had in my whole life!" It's true.

I had to drive to Minneapolis once, and I went on a back road just to see the country. But there was nothing to see. It's just flat and hot, and full of corn and soybeans and hogs. I remember one long, shimmering
40 stretch where I could see a couple of miles down the highway and there was a brown dot beside the road. As I got closer I saw it was a man sitting on a box by his front yard in some six-house town with a name like Spiggot or Urinal, watching my approach with inordinate interest. He watched me zip past and in the rearview mirror I could see him still
45 watching me going on down the road until at last I disappeared into a heat haze. The whole thing must have taken about five minutes. I wouldn't be surprised if even now he thinks of me from time to time.

He was wearing a baseball cap. You can always spot an Iowa man because he is wearing a baseball cap advertising John Deere or a feed
50 company, and because the back of his neck has been lasered into deep crevasses by years of driving a John Deere tractor back and forth in a blazing sun. (This does not do his mind a whole lot of good either.) His other distinguishing feature is that he looks ridiculous when he takes off his shirt because his neck and arms are chocolate brown and his
55 torso is as white as a sow's belly. In Iowa it is called a farmer's tan and it is, I believe, a badge of distinction.

Iowa women are almost always sensationally overweight—you see them at Merle Hay Mall in Des Moines on Saturdays, clammy and meaty in their shorts and halter-tops, looking a little like elephants dressed in
60 children's clothing, yelling at their kids, calling names like Dwayne and

Shauna. Jack Kerouac, of all people, thought that Iowa women were the prettiest in the country, but I don't think he ever went to Merle Hay Mall on a Saturday.

65   I don't think I would have stayed in Iowa. I never really felt at home there, even when I was small. In about 1957, my grandparents gave me a Viewmaster for my birthday and a packet of discs with the title "Iowa— Our Glorious State." I can remember thinking, even then, that the selection of glories was a trifle on the thin side. With no natural features of note, no national parks or battlefields or famous birthplaces, the View-

70   master people had to stretch their creative 3D talents to the full. Putting the Viewmaster to your eyes and clicking the white handle gave you, as I recall, a shot of Herbert Hoover's birthplace, impressively three-dimensional, followed by Iowa's other great treasure, the Little Brown Church in the Vale (which inspired the song whose tune nobody ever

75   quite knows), the highway bridge over the Mississippi River at Davenport (all the cars seemed to be hurrying towards Illinois), a field of waving corn, the bridge over the Missouri River at Council Bluffs and the Little Brown Church in the Vale again, taken from another angle. I can remember thinking even then that there must be more to life than that.

Excerpted from Bill Bryson, "Fat Girls in Des Moines," *Granta 23* (Cambridge, U.K.: Penguin Publishers, 1988).

Check Your Comprehension

1.   Why doesn't anyone leave Des Moines, according to Bryson?

2.   How does Bryson describe other Iowans—that is, the ones who are not from Des Moines?

3.   Why didn't Bryson ever feel at home in Iowa?

Vocabulary: Adverbs

Below is a list of adverbs ending in *-ly*. Choose the adverb that best fits in each of the sentences below. Use each one only once.

deliriously	faintly	impressively	hardly
sensationally	simultaneously	snidely	strangely

1.   _____ enough, I couldn't remember my brother's name.

2.   "Let's go to the park!" the twins said _____ .

3.   Joan had a bad cold, and spoke ———————— .

4.   He spoke ———————— ; I could ———————— hear him.

5.   The Empire State Building in New York City is ———————— tall.

6.   The *National Enquirer* presents its stories quite ———————— .

7.   The man was annoyed by the reporter's questions, and answered

very ———————— .

Think About It

1.   Des Moines, Iowa, has a population of 191,000. After reading this essay, did you think it was smaller? Why?

2.   The author uses several "made-up" names of small towns. What are they? Why do you think he used these invented names?

3.   As stated in the introduction to this reading, the author uses "hyperbole"—exaggeration. What examples can you find? Why do you think he uses exaggeration in them?

4.   Are there any similarities between the small-town life described here and small-town life in your own culture?

5.   Imagine you have just been selected as the head of the new Tourist Bureau of Lakey, a small American town. Lakey's town council has decided that it wants to attract more tourists to the town. Your job is to write a travel brochure that will be sent to people who may be interested in visiting the town.

Read the following information about Lakey, and then, with a partner or small group, put together your brochure. You may also use pictures if you wish.

Lakey
Population: 14,625
Location: Lost Oaks Valley
Elevation: 2,400 feet
Rivers: Lexington, Augustine
Wildlife: deer, squirrels, rabbits, and raccoons
History: Archeological evidence shows there was a prehistoric civilization there. The site of the town was inhabited by two Native American Indian tribes.
Current industry: ranching—goats, cattle, sheep
Museums: County Historical Museum, depicting life of the Indians and ranchers
Parks: Lost Oaks State Park, with camping, swimming and fishing facilities
10 restaurants, 1 hotel, 2 motels, 1 bed and breakfast inn

Synthesis

Discussion and Debate

1. Is size the only difference between a city and a town? What other factors might be included in this difference?

2. The readings in this chapter have presented generalizations or stereotypes of people in different regions or towns. Think about the region you and your family are from. Has it been stereotyped by "outside observers"? What is the stereotype? Is it accurate? Why or why not?

3. Competition between regions, cities, or countries is common throughout the world. What do you think causes this competition? What are the consequences of one group's stereotyping of another?

4. Think of another question to ask your classmates about the ideas presented in this chapter.

Writing Topics

1. Read the following topic sentences. Write two sentences supporting each of them.

   a. City life is exciting and interesting. _____

   _____

   _____

   b. Country life is slow and boring. _____

   _____

   _____

   c. City life is hectic and dangerous. _____

   _____

   _____

   d. Country life is peaceful and friendly. _____

   _____

   _____

2. Write a letter to a friend back home, describing the city or town you are living in in the United States. Include both the positive and negative aspects of life there.

3. Would you rather live in the city or the country? Write a short essay explaining your choice.

On Your Own

1. Choose a city in the United States that you would be interested in visiting someday. Write to the Chamber of Commerce of that city, requesting tourist information.

2. Interview two U.S.-born Americans from different parts of the United States. Ask them what it was like growing up there. (Or, ask one who grew up in a city and one who grew up in the country.) Take notes or tape record your interviews.

3. The following films deal with conflicts between regions or between city life and country life, or are good presentations of information about regions of the United States and their history. Check your local video store for any of the following:

   Town/City Conflict: *Crocodile Dundee, The Out-of-Towners, Continental Divide*

   Regional Conflict: *Annie Hall* (East vs. West Coast), *Mississippi Burning* (North vs. South)

   Regional Portrayal: *The Last Picture Show* (Texas), *Cross Creek* (north-central Florida lake country), *Fast Times at Ridgemont High* (California), *Wall Street* (New York)

4. Ask a U.S.-born friend to complete the following sentences.

   People from the North are ⸺⸺⸺⸺⸺⸺⸺⸺⸺ .

   People from the South are ⸺⸺⸺⸺⸺⸺⸺⸺⸺ .

   People from California are ⸺⸺⸺⸺⸺⸺⸺⸺⸺ .

   People from New York are ⸺⸺⸺⸺⸺⸺⸺⸺⸺ .

   People from the Midwest are ⸺⸺⸺⸺⸺⸺⸺⸺⸺ .

   People from small towns are ⸺⸺⸺⸺⸺⸺⸺⸺⸺ .

   People from cities are ⸺⸺⸺⸺⸺⸺⸺⸺⸺ .

   Compare the responses you got with those obtained by two of your classmates. What are the similarities and the differences?

6

Technology: The More Things Change

PART ONE
Computers: Mind versus Machine

Before You Read

Table 6.1   The Number of Personal Computers in Use, 1981–1987

Location	1981	1984	1987
Workplace	1,240,000	6,440,000	15,820,000
Schools	130,000	780,000	1,960,000
Home	750,000	11,950,000	19,970,000

Source: Bureau of the Census, *Statistical Abstract of the United States,
1989* (Washington, D.C., 1989), table 1308.

As shown by table 6.1, the use of computers in everyday life is
growing. The following article examines the effect on society that one
tiny invention—the silicon chip—has had. It also discusses some of the
long-term effects of the "computer revolution."

Before you read, think about the following questions:

• How has technology changed your daily life?

• What new "gadget" do you particularly like?

Glossary

SRI International   Research institute located in northern California

Luddites   People who believe that modern technology is out of
control and ruining the quality of life on Earth; they seek to limit
technology and its influence on the individual.

Martini   Cocktail usually made of gin and vermouth, served with an
olive; "a mean Martini" means a very good Martini.

About the Author

Merill Sheils is a writer for *Newsweek,* a weekly news magazine.

And Man Created the Chip
by Merill Sheils

Welcome! Always glad to show someone from the early '80s around the place. The biggest change, of course, is the smart machines— they're all around us. No need to be alarmed, they're very friendly. Can't imagine how you lived without them. The telephone, dear old
5 *thing, is giving a steady busy signal to a bill collector I'm avoiding. Unless he starts calling from a new number my phone doesn't know, he'll never get through. TURN OFF! Excuse me for shouting—almost forgot the bedroom television was on. Let's see, anything else before we go? The oven already knows the menu for tonight and the kitchen robot*
10 *will mix us a mean Martini. Guess we're ready. Oh no, you won't need a key. We'll just program the lock to recognize your voice and let you in whenever you want.*

A revolution is under way. Most Americans are already well aware of the gee-whiz gadgetry that is emerging, in rapidly accelerating bursts,
15 from the world's high-technology laboratories. But most of us perceive only dimly how pervasive and profound the changes of the next twenty years will be. We are at the dawn of the era of the smart machine—an "information age" that will change forever the way an entire nation works, plays, travels and even thinks. Just as the industrial revolution
20 dramatically expanded the strength of man's muscles and the reach of his hand, so the smart-machine revolution will magnify the power of his brain. But unlike the industrial revolution, which depended on finite re- sources such as iron and oil, a new information age will be fired by a seemingly limitless resource—the inexhaustible supply of knowledge
25 itself. Even computer scientists, who best understand the galloping technology and its potential, are wonderstruck by its implications. "It is really awesome," says L. C. Thomas of Bell Laboratories. "Every day is just as scary as the day before."

The driving force behind the revolution is the development of two
30 fundamental and interactive technologies—computers and integrated circuits. Today, tiny silicon chips half the size of a fingernail are etched with circuitry powerful enough to book seats on jumbo jets (and keep the planes working smoothly in the air), cut complex swatches of fabric with little wastage, help children learn to spell and play chess well
35 enough to beat all but the grandest masters. The new technology means that bits of computing power can be distributed wherever they might be useful—the way small electric motors have become ubiquitous—or

combined in giant mainframe computers to provide enormous problem-
solving potential. In addition, this "computational plenty" is making
40   smart machines easier to use and more forgiving of unskilled programming. Machines are even communicating with each other. "What's next?"
asks Peter E. Hart, director of SRI International's artificial-intelligence
center. "More to the point, what's *not* next?"

The explosion is just beginning. In 1979, the world market for
45   micro-electronics topped $11 billion. Over the next five years, chip
sales are expected to grow by at least 20 percent annually, and the market for microprocessors, entire "computers on a chip," will expand by
50 percent each year—even though the chips themselves and the computing power they represent are diving in price. As industry officials are
50   fond of remarking, if the automobile industry had improved its technology at the same rate computer science has, it would now be turning out
Rolls Royces that cost no more than $70 apiece.

There are a few clouds on the industry's horizon: capital costs are
rising, and Japan is mounting an all-out challenge to American suprem-
55   acy in the field. Some experts predict that the shape of the industry will
change considerably by the end of the decade, perhaps even shrinking
down to a half-dozen IBM-like giants. But whatever shake-outs lie
ahead, the world will continue to snap up chips as fast as manufacturers can turn them out, creating a mushrooming "information indus-
60   try" that will grow into a $500 billion-a-year enterprise, by far the big-
gest on earth.

The transformation will not be easy, for smart machines bring with
them the seeds of widespread economic dislocation and social unrest.
Eventually, for example, they will make possible the full automation of
65   many factories, displacing millions of blue-collar workers with a new
"steel-collar" class. Even office workers will feel the crunch, as smart
machines do more and more of the clerical work. Traditional busi-
nesses such as television networks and publishing companies will en-
counter new competition as programmers and advertisers beam infor-
70   mation directly into the consumer's home.

Some social critics warn of a new generation of Luddites who will
fight to stop the new technology through restrictive laws—or even sabo-
tage. Others predict the rise of a new criminal class of master computer-
raiders. And many view the advent of smart machines with a dread they
75   cannot really explain. To them, computers are alien, too complicated to
understand and too prone to horrifying mistakes like the recent false
alarms on the Air Force's NORAD missile-detection system. Alarmists
harbor fears that the technology will get out of control—perhaps pro-
ducing new machines that can outsmart their human masters.

80   But industry experts think these problems can—and will—be solved.
In the optimists' scenario, educational programs will retrain displaced

workers and equip them with skills suited to the booming new information business. Meanwhile, laymen will grow more and more comfortable with computers as they invade everyday life. And in the end, the
85 smart-machine revolution will do far more to enrich life than most Americans realize. As the industry likes to picture the future, the new technology offers potential solutions to humanity's most intractable problems—the allocation of energy resources, food enough for all and the worldwide improvement of health care, to name just a few.

90   Somewhere between the dire warnings and the utopian visions, the future will take form. But there is no doubt that the era of smart machines will be vastly different from anything that preceded it. "What we are doing is creating a new class structure around wealth—this time, the wealth of information," says SRI International futurologist Peter
95 Schwartz. "Like today's 'haves and have-nots,' we will be a society of the 'knows and know-nots.'"

Excerpted from Merill Sheils, "And Man Created the Chip," *Newsweek*, June 30, 1980.

Check Your Comprehension

1. Who is speaking in the first paragraph?

2. According to the author, what is the relationship between the Industrial Revolution and the next "revolution"?

3. What negative effects might "smart machines" have on society, according to this reading?

4. What are the two different visions of technology's role and influence on the future, as presented in this article?

Vocabulary: More Latin Words

The table below contains Latin-based stems, prefixes, and suffixes of English words. In each box, write three different words that contain the word part at the top of the box. An example is given in the first box.

volv	vade	auto
1. *revolve*	1.	1.
2.	2.	2.
3.	3.	3.
cept	**strict**	**tract**
1.	1.	1.
2.	2.	2.
3.	3.	3.
loc	**com**	**able**
1.	1.	1.
2.	2.	2.
3.	3.	3.

Think About It

1. What are some of the latest "gee-whiz" gadgets that consumers can buy? Do you think they will change the average lifestyle?

2. The author says that industry officials like to say that if the automobile industry were as up to date as the computer industry, Rolls-Royce cars would cost $70. Do you think this is true? Why?

3. What do you think of the Luddite philosophy? Do you think it is realistic in today's society?

4. Recent new technologies include

    • "Caller ID," which allows a person to identify the person calling on the telephone by showing the phone number of that person

    • pocket-sized copiers the size of a package of cigarettes with which you can scan and make copies of pages from books and magazines

    Invent a new technological device that people could use in their daily lives. Write a short description of your new invention, and draw a sketch of it, if possible. Explain your invention to your classmates.

ROTHCO

"BEEN HERE LONG?"

Before You Read

Not everyone is happy with technological developments. The author of this reading explains why he believes that personal computers are not beneficial to society.

Before you read, think about the following questions:

- Have you learned to use a computer? Why or why not?
- Do you fear the power of computers?

About the Author

Wendell Berry was born in 1934 in rural Kentucky, where he also attended college. He is, as this reading indicates, a farmer as well as a writer concerned with the environment.

Why I Won't Buy a Computer

by Wendell Berry

Like almost everybody else, I am hooked to the energy corporations, which I do not admire. I hope to become less hooked to them. In my work, I try to be as little hooked to them as possible. As a farmer, I do almost all of my work with horses. As a writer, I work with a pencil
5 or a pen and a piece of paper.

My wife types my work on a Royal standard typewriter bought new in 1956 and as good now as it was then. As she types, she sees things that are wrong and marks them with small checks in the margins. She is my best critic because she is the one most familiar with my habitual
10 errors and weaknesses. She also understands, sometimes better than I do, what *ought* to be said. We have, I think, a literary cottage industry that works well and pleasantly. I do not see anything wrong with it.

A number of people, by now, have told me that I would greatly improve things by buying a computer. My answer is that I am not going to
15 do it. I have several reasons, and they are good ones.

The first is the one I mentioned at the beginning. I would hate to think that my work as a writer could not be done without direct dependence on strip-mined coal. How could I conscientiously write against the rape of nature if I were, in the act of writing, implicated in the rape?
20 For the same reason, it matters to me that my writing is done in the daytime without electric light.

I do not admire the computer manufacturers a great deal more than I admire the energy industries. I have seen their advertisements, attempting to seduce struggling or failing farmers into the belief that they
25 can solve their problems by buying yet another piece of expensive equipment. I do not see that computers are bringing us one step nearer to anything that does matter to me: peace, economic justice, ecological health, political honesty, family and community, stability, good work.

What would a computer cost me? More money, for one thing, than I
30 can afford, and more than I wish to pay to people whom I do not admire. But the cost would not be just monetary. It is well understood that technological innovation always requires the discarding of the "old model"—the "old model" in this case being not just our old Royal standard, but my wife, my critic, my closest reader, my fellow worker. Thus (and I
35 think this is typical of present-day technological innovation), what would be superseded would be not only something, but somebody. In order to be technologically up-to-date as a writer, I would have to sacrifice an association that I am dependent upon and that I treasure.

My final and perhaps my best reason for not owning a computer is that I do not wish to fool myself. I disbelieve, and therefore strongly resent, the assertion that I or anybody else could write better or more easily with a computer than with a pencil.

To make myself as plain as I can, I should give my standards for technological innovation in my own work. They are as follows:

45   1. The new tool should be cheaper than the one it replaces.

2. It should be at least as small in scale as the one it replaces.

3. It should do work that it is clearly and demonstrably better than the one it replaces.

4. It should use less energy than the one it replaces.

50   5. If possible, it should use some form of solar energy, such as that of the body.

6. It should be repairable by a person of ordinary intelligence, provided that he or she has the necessary tools.

7. It should be purchasable and repairable as near to home as possible.

8. It should come from a small, privately owned shop or store that will take it back for maintenance and repair.

9. It should not replace or disrupt anything good that already exists, and this includes family and community relationships.

From *Bread Loaf Quarterly/New England Review* (Autumn 1987).

Check Your Comprehension

1. Why doesn't the author admire either the energy corporations or computer manufacturers?

2. What does the author think a computer would "cost" him?

3. Given the author's "standards for technological innovation," what other new tools do you think he might object to?

Vocabulary: Related Nouns and Verbs

Many nouns and verbs have forms that are identical. For example:

> Many power companies *mine* coal. (*verb*)
> They found the coal in a *mine.* (*noun*)

Others have different, but related forms.

> I don't know where to *begin.* (*verb*)
> Why don't you start at the *beginning?* (*noun*)

For each of the nouns or verbs in the table below, give the corresponding noun or verb. In some cases, there may not be a related word. In that case, place an asterisk (*) in the space.

	VERBS	NOUNS
a.	admire	_____
b.	_____	answer
c.	_____	assertion
d.	criticize	_____
e.	_____	disbelief
f.	discard	_____
g.	disrupt	_____
h.	_____	error
i.	_____	honesty
j.	hook	_____
k.	_____	mark
l.	_____	model
m.	own	_____
n.	purchase	_____
o.	_____	reason
p.	require	_____
q.	resent	_____
r.	_____	sacrifice
s.	_____	technology
t.	write	_____

Think About It

1. One reason Berry says he doesn't want a computer is that his wife would no longer be included in his work. Do you think he is right? Why or why not?

2. Berry claims his reasons for not wanting a computer are "good ones." Do you agree? Which are good and which are not, in your opinion?

3. Many people have disagreed with Mr. Berry, saying that modern inventions are "labor-saving" devices. Without them, they argue, people remain slaves to boring, repetitive work. Do you agree? What do you think life was like before labor-saving inventions, such as clothes washers, vacuum cleaners, or dishwashers?

4. What is the relationship between the cartoon at the beginning of this section and the reading?

5. Mr. Berry uses horses instead of farm machinery, and a typewriter instead of a computer. He also says he works during the day, so that he does not have to use electric light. With a partner, list ten other modern inventions used in daily life. Then, using his nine rules for technological innovation, think of a substitute for that invention. List the replacement's advantages and disadvantages as well.

INVENTION	REPLACEMENT	ADVANTAGE	DISADVANTAGE
telephone	*writing letters*	*costs less*	*not useful in emergencies; too slow*
1. _____	_____	_____	_____
		_____	_____
2. _____	_____	_____	_____
		_____	_____
3. _____	_____	_____	_____
		_____	_____
4. _____	_____	_____	_____
		_____	_____
5. _____	_____	_____	_____
		_____	_____
6. _____	_____	_____	_____
		_____	_____
7. _____	_____	_____	_____
		_____	_____
8. _____	_____	_____	_____
		_____	_____
9. _____	_____	_____	_____
		_____	_____
10. _____	_____	_____	_____
		_____	_____

PART TWO
The Nuclear Age: Life with the Bomb

Before You Read

Table 6.2   U.S. and Soviet Strategic Nuclear Forces, End of 1987

Type	Number of Launchers	Number of Warheads	Total Megatons
United States			
ICBMs	1,000	2,310	1,043.7
SLBMs	640	5,632	409.6
Bombers/weapons	361	5,070	1,593.9
Grand Total	2,001	13,012	3,047.2
Soviet Union			
ICBMs	1,392	6,846	3,841.2
SLBMs	928	3,232	1,770.0
Bombers/weapons	155	1,170	808.0
Grand Total	2,475	11,248	6,419.2

ICBM = intercontinental ballistic missile
SLBM = submarine-launched ballistic missile
Source: Adapted from *Bulletin of the Atomic Scientists*, 1988. Published by Educational Foundation for Nuclear Science, 6042 S. Kimbark Ave., Chicago, Ill. 60637.

The following reading is actually portions of two speeches about nuclear arms: one by Ronald Reagan, and one by Mikhail Gorbachev. Both leaders speak of technology, peace, and the future.

Before you read, think about the following questions:

- What are relations like between the United States and Russia today?

- Do you feel threatened or more secure knowing that there are nuclear weapons in the world?

Glossary

Krashnoyarsk (also spelled *Krasnoyarsk*)   City in Russia that is the site of a large radar installation; it has been the subject of controversy between the United States and the USSR.

Reykjavik   Capital city of Iceland, where the leaders of the United States and the USSR met in 1986 to discuss nuclear disarmament

About the Authors

Ronald Reagan was the 40th president of the United States, serving two terms (eight years). At the time of this writing, Mikhail Gorbachev has been the leader of the Soviet Union since 1985. The title of the office he holds changed from general secretary of the Communist Party of the USSR to president of the USSR in 1988.

Two Speeches on Nuclear Disarmament
Ronald Reagan and Mikhail Gorbachev

Nuclear Disarmament and SDI
Ronald Reagan, President of the United States, October 13, 1986

Before I report on our talks though, allow me to set the stage by explaining two things that were very much a part of our talks, one a
5 treaty and the other a defense against nuclear missiles which we are trying to develop. You've heard their titles a thousand times—the ABM treaty and SDI. Those letters stand for anti-ballistic missile and Strategic Defense Initiative.

Some years ago, the US and the Soviet Union agreed to limit any
10 defense against nuclear missile attacks to the emplacement in one location in each country of a small number of missiles capable of intercepting and shooting down incoming nuclear missiles. Thus leaving our real defense a policy called the Mutual Assured Destruction, meaning if one side launched a nuclear attack, the other side could retaliate. This mu-
15 tual threat of destruction was believed to be a deterrent against either side striking first.

So here we sit with thousands of nuclear warheads targeted on each other and capable of wiping out both our countries. The Soviets deployed the few anti-ballistic missiles around Moscow as the treaty
20 permitted. Our country didn't bother deploying because the threat of nationwide annihilation made such limited defense seem useless.

For some years now we have been aware that the Soviets have been developing a nationwide defense. They have installed a large modern radar at Krashnoyarsk which we believe is a critical part of a radar sys-
25 tem designed to provide radar guidance for anti-ballistic missiles protecting the entire nation. This is a violation of the ABM treaty.

Believing that a policy of mutual destruction and slaughter of their citizens and ours was uncivilized, I asked our military a few years ago to study and see if there was a practical way to destroy nuclear missiles
30 after their launch but before they can reach their targets rather than

just destroy people. This is the goal for what we call SDI, and our scientists researching such a system are convinced it is practical and that several years down the road we can have such a system ready to deploy.

Yesterday, Sunday morning, Mr. Gorbachev and I, with our foreign
35 ministers, came together again and took up the report of our teams. It was most promising. The Soviets had asked for a 10-year-delay in the deployment of SDI programs. In an effort to see how we could satisfy their concern while protecting our principles and security, we proposed a 10-year period in which we began with the reduction of all strategic
40 nuclear arms, bombers, air-launched cruise missiles, intercontinental ballistic missiles, submarine launched ballistic missiles and the weapons they carry.

They would be reduced 50 percent in the first five years. During the next five years, we would continue by eliminating all remaining offen-
45 sive ballistic missiles of all ranges. During that time we would proceed with research, development and testing of SDI. All done in conformity with ABM provisions. At the 10-year point, with all ballistic missiles eliminated, we could proceed to deploy advanced defenses, at the same time permitting the Soviets to do likewise.
50 Here the debate began. The General Secretary wanted wording that in effect would have kept us from developing the SDI for the entire 10 years. In effect, he was killing SDI and unless I agreed, all that work toward eliminating nuclear weapons would go down the drain— canceled.
55 I told him that I had pledged to the American people that I would not trade away SDI—there was no way I could tell our people their Government would not protect them against nuclear destruction. I went to Reykjavik determined that everything was negotiable except two things, our freedom and our future.
60 I am still optimistic that a way will be found. The door is open and the opportunity to begin eliminating the nuclear threat is within reach.

USSR Arms Reduction
Mikhail Gorbachev, Prime Minister of the Soviet Union,
December 7, 1988

65 What will humanity be like as it enters the 21st century? Thoughts about this already very near future are engaging people's minds. While we look forward to the future with the anticipation of change for the better, we also view it with alarm.

Today, the world is a very different place from what it was at the
70 beginning of this century, and even in the middle of it. And the world and all of its components keep changing.

The emergence of nuclear weapons is a tragic way of stressing the fundamental nature of these changes. Being the material symbol and the bearer of the ultimate military force, nuclear weapons at the same
75 time laid bare the absolute limits of this force.

Humankind is faced with the problem of survival, of self-protection, in all its magnitude.

As regards space exploration in general, the outlines of future industry in space are becoming increasingly clear.
80   The Soviet position on this point is known only too well: any activities in space must exclude deployment of any weapons there. For that, too, we need a legal base which, in fact, is already established by the 1967 [ABM] Treaty, and by other agreements.

Even so, there is a pressing need to develop a comprehensive regime
85 for peaceful activity in space. As for control over the observance of that regime, that would be a prerogative of a World Space Organization.

We have proposed the establishment of such an organization on many occasions. In fact, we are prepared to include in its network our radar station at Krasnoyarsk. The decision to hand this station over to
90 the USSR Academy of Sciences has already been made.

And now for the most important thing of all, without which no other issue of the forthcoming age can be solved, that is, disarmament.

International developments and affairs have been distorted by the arms race and the militarization of thought.
95   As you will no doubt be aware, on January 15, 1986, the Soviet Union advanced a program to construct a world free from nuclear weapons. Efforts to translate this program into negotiations already have produced some tangible results.

Tomorrow will be the first anniversary of the signing of the Treaty
100 on the Elimination of Intermediate-Range and Shorter Range Missiles. And I am pleased to say today that the implementation of the Treaty— the destruction of missiles—is proceeding normally, in an atmosphere of trust and constructive work.

A large breach has been made in the wall of suspicion and hostility,
105 which once seemed to be impenetrable. And we are witnessing a new historic reality: the principle of excessive arms stockpiling is giving way to the principle of reasonable sufficiency for defense.

We are witnessing the first efforts to build a new model of security through the reduction of armaments on the basis of compromise, not
110 through their build-up, as was almost always the case in the past.

And the Soviet leadership has decided once again to demonstrate its willingness to encourage this healthy process not only in words but in actions.

Today I am able to inform you of the fact that the Soviet Union has
115 decided to reduce its armed forces.

The USSR and the United States have built up immense nuclear-missile arsenals. But they have also managed to clearly acknowledge the responsibility and become the first to conclude an agreement on the reduction and physical elimination of some of those weapons, which
120   have threatened their own countries and all the other nations of the world.

And I hope our joint efforts to end the epoch of wars, confrontation and regional conflicts, to end aggression against Nature, the terror of hunger and poverty and political terrorism will justify our aspirations.
125   This is our common goal and we shall be able to achieve it only by working together.

From *Vital Speeches of the Day,* vol. 53 (Nov. 15, 1986), vol. 54 (May 1, 1988).

Check Your Comprehension

1.   Explain what the letters ABM and SDI stand for. What is Mutual Assured Destruction?

2.   What explanation does Reagan give of why the United States did not deploy any ABMs?

3.   What is the Soviet Union's attitude toward SDI?

4.   What does Gorbachev mean when he says "a large breach has been made in the wall of suspicion and hostility" (line 98)?

Vocabulary: Military Words

Choose one verb and one noun from the columns below, and write a sentence (top of next page) using both. Use each word only once.

VERBS	NOUNS
deploy	aggression
deter	annihilation
eliminate	arsenal
implement	disarmament
negotiate	emplacement
retaliate	hostility
stockpile	regime
threaten	terrorism

1. _____
2. _____
3. _____
4. _____
5. _____
6. _____
7. _____
8. _____

Think About It

1. Do you think that SDI is a good or a bad idea? Why?

2. Do you think the policy of mutual assured destruction has been a successful one? Why or why not?

3. How do you think the world would be different today if there were no nuclear weapons?

4. How has the world changed since these speeches were given?

5. Continue the dialogue below, in which Mr. Reagan and Mr. Gorbachev debate SDI.

   MR. GORBACHEV: *The Soviet position is clear. Any activities in space must exclude deployment of any weapons there.*

   MR. REAGAN: *I have pledged to the American people that I will not trade away SDI. We must protect our people against nuclear destruction.*

   MR. GORBACHEV:

Before You Read

Table 6.3   Robot Manufacture, 1985–1987

	Number Shipped			Value (mil. $)		
Item	1985	1986	1987	1985	1986	1987
Complete robots	5,466	6,673	4,273	275.7	274.6	187.5
Robot accessories and parts	×	×	×	69.5	71.4	62.4

Source: Bureau of the Census, *Statistical Abstract of the United States, 1989* (Washington, D.C., 1989), table 1304.

The next reading is a short story that portrays the author's vision of technology in the future, as well as the potential effect of nuclear weapons on everyday life.

Before you read, think about the following questions:

• Do you think it is possible to survive a nuclear war?

• What would the world be like after a major nuclear war?

Glossary

Sara Teasdale   Twentieth-century American lyric poet

Picassos and Matisses   Paintings by the artists Pablo Picasso and Henri Matisse

Baal   Ancient Phoenician god of the sun

About the Author

Ray Bradbury was born in 1920 in the state of Illinois. He moved to Los Angeles as a teenager and has spent most of his life there. He began writing science-fiction and fantasy stories for magazines, and his reputation grew after the publication of his famous collection of stories called *The Martian Chronicles*. He has written drama, fiction, and poetry, but is best known for his science fiction, including the novels *Fahrenheit 451* and *Something Wicked This Way Comes* and the story collection *The Illustrated Man*.

August 2026: There Will Come Soft Rains

by Ray Bradbury

In the living room the voice-clock sang, *Tick-tock, seven o'clock, time to get up, time to get up, seven o'clock!* as if it were afraid that nobody would. The morning house lay empty. The clock ticked on, repeating and repeating its sound into the emptiness. *Seven-nine, break-*
5 *fast time, seven-nine!*

In the kitchen the breakfast stove gave a hissing sigh and ejected from its warm interior eight pieces of perfectly browned toast, eight eggs sunnyside up, sixteen slices of bacon, two coffees, and two cool glasses of milk.

10 "Today is August 4, 2026," said a second voice from the kitchen ceiling, "in the city of Allendale, California." It repeated the date three times for memory's sake. "Today is Mr. Featherstone's birthday. Today is the anniversary of Tilita's marriage. Insurance is payable, as are the water, gas, and light bills."

15 Somewhere in the walls, relays clicked, memory tapes glided under electric eyes.

Eight-one, eight-one o'clock, off to school, off to work, run, run, eight-one! But no doors slammed, no carpets took the soft tread of rubber heels. It was raining outside. The weather box on the front door
20 sang quietly: "Rain, rain, go away; rubbers, raincoats for today . . ." and the rain tapped on the empty house, echoing.

Outside, the garage chimed and lifted its door to reveal the waiting car. After a long wait the door swung down again.

At eight-thirty the eggs were shriveled and the toast was like stone.
25 An aluminum wedge scraped them into the sink, where hot water whirled them down a metal throat which digested and flushed them away to the distant sea. The dirty dishes were dropped into a hot washer and emerged twinkling dry.

Nine-fifteen, sang the clock, *time to clean.*
30 Out of the warrens in the wall, tiny robot mice darted. The rooms were acrawl with the small cleaning animals, all rubber and metal. They thudded against chairs, whirling their mustached runners, kneading the rug nap, sucking gently at hidden dust. Then, like mysterious invaders, they popped into their burrows. Their pink electric eyes faded. The
35 house was clean.

Ten o'clock. The sun came out from behind the rain. The house stood alone in a city of rubble and ashes. This was the one house left standing. At night the ruined city gave off a radioactive glow which could be seen for miles.

40   *Ten-fifteen.* The garden sprinklers whirled up in golden founts, fill-
ing the soft morning air with scatterings of brightness. The water pelted
windowpanes, running down the charred west side where the house
had been burned evenly free of its white paint. The entire west face of
the house was black, save for five places. Here the silhouette in paint of
45 a man mowing a lawn. Here, as in a photograph, a woman bent to pick
flowers. Still farther over, their images burned on wood in one titanic
instant, a small boy, hands flung into the air; higher up, the image of a
thrown ball, and opposite him a girl, hands raised to catch a ball which
never came down.

50   The five spots of paint—the man, the woman, the children, the
ball—remained. The rest was a thin charcoaled layer.

     The gentle sprinkler rain filled the garden with falling light.

     Until this day, how well the house had kept its peace. How carefully
it had inquired, "Who goes there? What's the password?" and, getting
55 no answer from lonely foxes and whining cats, it had shut up its windows and drawn shades in an old-maidenly preoccupation with self-
protection which bordered on a mechanical paranoia.

     It quivered at each sound, the house did. If a sparrow brushed a
window, the shade snapped up. The bird, startled, flew off! No, not even
60 a bird must touch the house!

     The house was an altar with ten thousand attendants, big, small,
servicing, attending, in choirs. But the gods had gone away, and the ritual of the religion continued senselessly, uselessly.

     Twelve noon.
65   A dog whined, shivering, on the front porch.

     The front door recognized the dog voice and opened. The dog, once
huge and fleshy, but now gone to bone and covered with sores, moved
in and through the house, tracking mud. Behind it whirred angry mice,
angry at having to pick up mud, angry at inconvenience.

70   For not a leaf fragment blew under the door but what the wall panels flipped open and copper scrap rats flashed swiftly out. The offend-
ing dust, hair, or paper, seized in miniature steel jaws, was raced back
to the burrows. There, down tubes which fed into the cellar, it was
dropped into the sighing vent of an incinerator which sat like evil Baal
75 in a dark corner.

     The dog ran upstairs, hysterically yelping to each door, at last real-
izing, as the house realized, that only silence was here.

     It sniffed the air and scratched the kitchen door. Behind the door,
the stove was making pancakes which filled the house with a rich baked
80 odor and the scent of maple syrup.

     The dog frothed at the mouth, lying at the door, sniffing, its eyes
turned to fire. It ran wildly in circles, biting at its tail, spun in a frenzy,
and died. It lay in the parlor for an hour.

Two o'clock, sang a voice.

85 Delicately sensing decay at last, the regiments of mice hummed out as softly as blown gray leaves in an electrical wind.

Two-fifteen.

The dog was gone.

In the cellar, the incinerator glowed suddenly and a whirl of sparks

90 leaped up the chimney.

Two thirty-five.

Bridge tables sprouted from patio walls. Playing cards fluttered onto pads in a shower of pips. Martinis manifested on an oaken bench with egg-salad sandwiches. Music played.

95 But the tables were silent and the cards untouched.

At four o'clock the tables folded like great butterflies back through the paneled walls.

Four-thirty.

The nursery walls glowed.

100 Animals took shape: yellow giraffes, blue lions, pink antelopes, lilac panthers cavorting in crystal substance. The walls were glass. They looked out upon color and fantasy. Hidden films clicked through well-oiled sprockets, and the walls lived. The nursery floor was woven to resemble a crisp, cereal meadow. Over this ran aluminum roaches and

105 iron crickets, and in the hot still air butterflies of delicate red tissue wavered among the sharp aroma of animal spoors! There was the sound like a great matted yellow hive of bees within a dark bellows, the lazy bumble of a purring lion. And there was a patter of okapi feet and the murmur of a fresh jungle rain, like other hoofs, falling upon the summer-

110 starched grass. Now the walls dissolved into distances of parched weed, mile on mile, and warm endless sky. The animals drew away into thorn brakes and water holes.

It was the children's hour.

Five o'clock. The bath filled with clear hot water.

115 *Six, seven, eight o'clock.* The dinner dishes manipulated like magic tricks, and in the study a click. In the metal stand opposite the hearth where a fire now blazed up warmly, a cigar popped out, half an inch of soft gray ash on it, smoking, waiting.

Nine o'clock. The beds warmed their hidden circuits, for nights

120 were cool here.

Nine-five. A voice spoke from the study ceiling:

"Mrs. McClellan, which poem would you like this evening?"

The house was silent.

The voice said at last, "Since you express no preference, I shall se-

125 lect a poem at random." Quiet music rose to back the voice. "Sara Teasdale. As I recall, your favorite. . . .

There will come soft rains and the smell of the ground,
And swallows circling with their shimmering sound;

And frogs in the pools singing at night,
130   And wild plum trees in tremulous white;

Robins will wear their feathery fire,
Whistling their whims on a low fence-wire;

And not one will know of the war, not one
Will care at last when it is done.

135   Not one would mind, neither bird nor tree,
If mankind perished utterly;

And Spring herself, when she woke at dawn
Would scarcely know that we were gone.

The fire burned on the stone hearth and the cigar fell away into a
140   mound of quiet ash on its tray. The empty chairs faced each other between the silent walls, and the music played.

At ten o'clock the house began to die.

The wind blew. A falling tree bough crashed through the kitchen
window. Cleaning solvent, bottled, shattered over the stove. The room
145   was ablaze in an instant!

"Fire!" screamed a voice. The house lights flashed, water pumps
shot water from the ceilings. But the solvent spread on the linoleum,
licking, eating, under the kitchen door, while the voices took it up in
chorus: "Fire, fire, fire!"

150   The house tried to save itself. Doors sprang tightly shut, but the
windows were broken by the heat and the wind blew and sucked upon
the fire.

The house gave ground as the fire in ten billion angry sparks moved
with flaming ease from room to room and then up the stairs. While
155   scurrying water rats squeaked from the walls, pistoled their water, and
ran for more. And the wall sprays let down showers of mechanical rain.

But too late. Somewhere, sighing, a pump shrugged to a stop. The
quenching rain ceased. The reserve water supply which had filled baths
and washed dishes for many quiet days was gone.

160   The fire crackled up the stairs. It fed upon Picassos and Matisses in
the upper halls, like delicacies, baking off the oil flesh, tenderly crisping
the canvases into black shavings.

Now the fire lay in beds, stood in windows, changed the colors of
drapes!

165   And then, reinforcements.

From attic trapdoors, blind robot faces peered down with faucet
mouths gushing green chemical.

The fire backed off, as even an elephant must at the sight of a dead
snake. Now there were twenty snakes whipping over the floor, killing
170   the fire with a clear cold venom of green froth.

But the fire was clever. It had sent flame outside the house, up through the attic to the pumps there. An explosion! The attic brain which directed the pumps was shattered into bronze shrapnel on the beams.

175   The fire rushed back into every closet and felt of the clothes hung there.

The house shuddered, oak bone on bone, its bared skeleton cringing from the heat, its wire, its nerves revealed as if a surgeon had torn the skin off to let the red veins and capillaries quiver in the scalded air. 180 Help, help! Fire, fire, run, run, like a tragic nursery rhyme, a dozen voices, high, low, like children dying in a forest, alone, alone. And the voices fading as the wires popped their sheathings like hot chestnuts. One, two, three, four, five voices died.

In the nursery the jungle burned. Blue lions roared, purple giraffes 185 bounded off. The panthers ran in circles, changing color, and ten million animals, running before the fire, vanished off toward a distant steaming river. . . .

Ten more voices died. In the last instant under the fire avalanche, other choruses, oblivious, could be heard announcing the time, playing 190 music, cutting the lawn by remote-control mower, or setting an umbrella frantically out and in, the slamming and opening front door, a thousand things happening, like a clock shop when each clock strikes the hour insanely before or after the other, a scene of maniac confusion, yet unity; singing, screaming, a few last cleaning mice darting 195 bravely out to carry the horrid ashes away! And one voice, with sublime disregard for the situation, read poetry aloud in the fiery study, until all the film spools burned, until all the wires withered and the circuits cracked.

The fire burst the house and let it slam flat down, puffing out skirts 200 of spark and smoke.

In the kitchen, an instant before the rain of fire and timber, the stove could be seen making breakfasts at a psychopathic rate, ten dozen eggs, six loaves of toast, twenty dozen bacon strips, which, eaten by fire, started the stove working again, hysterically hissing!

205   The crash. The attic smashing into kitchen and parlor. The parlor into cellar, cellar into sub-cellar. Deep freeze, armchair, film tapes, circuits, beds, and all like skeletons thrown in a cluttered mound deep under.

Smoke and silence. A great quantity of smoke.

210   Dawn showed faintly in the east. Among the ruins, one wall stood alone. Within the wall, a last voice said, over and over again and again, even as the sun rose to shine upon the heaped rubble and steam:

"Today is August 5, 2026, today is August 5, 2026, today is . . . ."

From Ray Bradbury, "August 2026: There Will Come Soft Rains," *Colliers*, 1950, vol. 5.

Check Your Comprehension

1. How many people lived in the house in this story? What's the *first* clue that tells you this? What has happened to them?
2. How does the poem by Sara Teasdale relate to the story?
3. Who is the main character of this story?
4. What can this house do? What is it not able to do?

Vocabulary: Literary Language

The language used in literature—stories and poems—is usually different from that found in magazine or other articles. Why do you think this is true? Read the sentences below, and then write them in "plain English"—that is, use simpler vocabulary, and change the syntax where necessary.

> EXAMPLE: *But no doors slammed, no carpets took the soft tread of rubber heels.*
> No one slammed any doors, no one walked on the carpets.

1. The rooms were acrawl with the small cleaning animals, all rubber and metal.

_____

_____

_____

_____

2. Until this day, how well the house had kept its peace. How carefully it had inquired, "Who goes there? What's the password?" and, getting no answer from lonely foxes and whining cats, it had shut up its windows and drawn shades in an old-maidenly preoccupation with self-protection which bordered on a mechanical paranoia.

_____

_____

_____

_____

_____

3. For not a leaf fragment blew under the door but what the wall panels flipped open and copper scrap rats flashed swiftly out.

_____

_____

4.   The house was an altar with ten thousand attendants, big, small, servicing, attending, in choirs. But the gods had gone away, and the ritual of the religion continued senselessly, uselessly.

_____

_____

5.   The house gave ground as the fire in ten billion angry sparks moved with flaming ease from room to room and then up the stairs.

_____

_____

Think About It

1.   Did you like this story? Why or why not?
2.   Why do you think Ray Bradbury wrote this story? What "message" did he want to relate?
3.   Imagine that it is the day after a nuclear war. Somehow, your house has been spared from destruction. Inside, you and your family have enough food for 30 days. The surviving government officials say they can *probably* rescue you in 25 days.
     Outside, there are five of your neighbors who have survived as well—however, their homes have not. They have no food or shelter. You, along with your family, must decide whether you will let any of them into your house to share your food. With your group, vote on which, if any, of the following neighbors you will share your food with. Then answer the questions following these descriptions.
     a. Tommy, a 12-year-old boy. His parents were both killed, and he is injured very badly.
     b. Dr. Jones, a 60-year-old retired surgeon
     c. Mrs. Leonard, a 35-year-old woman who is expecting a baby
     d. Miss Thomas, a beautiful and famous movie star, 22 years old
     e. Mr. Burke, a strong 30-year-old carpenter. His wife and mother survived because they were in another country visiting relatives. They are still in that country.

     Now, answer these questions and report your decisions to the class.
     a. Will you let anyone in to share your food? Why or why not?
     b. Whom will you let in? Why did you choose that person or persons?
     c. Whom won't you let in? Why?

Synthesis

Discussion and Debate

1. In your opinion, are we currently living in a time of war or a time of peace? Why do you feel that way?

2. Technology has given us the ability to explore space. Do you think space exploration is important? What purpose does it serve?

3. Much criticism of new technology comes from older generations. Why do you think this is the case? Why do you think younger people seem to adapt more easily to new technologies?

4. Think of another question to ask your classmates about the ideas presented in this chapter.

Writing Topics

1. Imagine that you are an alien from another planet, visiting Earth for the first time. Write a report to the people of your planet, explaining three of the "strange" things you have found on Earth.

2. Do you think that we should develop more weapons and weapons technology or less? Write a letter to the president of the United States expressing your opinion on weapons development. (If you wish, mail your letter, and report to the class on the response.)

3. In either a short essay or a short story, write a description of daily life in the year 2050. Choose one aspect of life, such as school or work, as the main focus.

On Your Own

1. Go to a computer store to gather information about different personal computers. Collect any brochures and price lists they have. Choose which computer you will buy, based on the information you have gotten.

2. Look at a current issue of a magazine that deals with science and technology (for example, *Omni*, *Discover*, or *Scientific American*). Find an article that interests you and read it. Report on the article to your classmates.

3. Read a short science-fiction story written by Ray Bradbury or Isaac Asimov (or another author of your choice, if you know of one). What is his or her vision of the future or technology?

4. There are many films that deal with space, technology, the future, or nuclear war. Check your local video store for any of the following:

Dr. Strangelove   *2001: A Space Odyssey*   *Silkwood*
The China Syndrome   *Modern Problems*
Strange Tales/Ray Bradbury Theater

7
Current Problems: Fool's Paradise

PART ONE
Homelessness: Home Sweet Home

Before You Read

Figure 7.1   Public Housing Units, 1960–1987

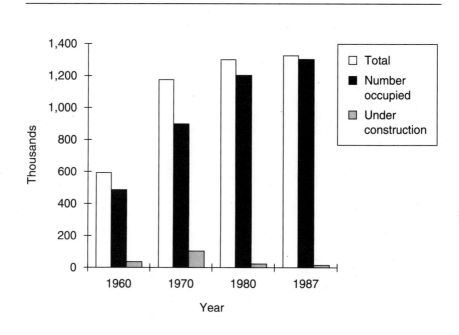

Source: Bureau of the Census, *Statistical Abstract of the United States, 1989* (Washington, D.C., 1989), table 1257.

In this reading, the author discusses briefly what he thinks are some of the causes of a major American problem—homelessness. He then explains what ordinary people can do to help solve the problem.

Before you read, think about the following questions:

- Have you seen homeless people in your city, or any city you have visited? How did it make you feel?

- How do you think people become homeless?

Glossary

Yuppies   Taken from the initial letters of "young urban professionals," a term referring to generally wealthy young city-dwellers

gentrification   Improvement and rehabilitation of an old area of a
city, usually causing rents to rise and the population to change

What We Can Do About the Homeless
by Charles Whitaker

Homelessness has grown at a dramatic rate in the last decade,
alarming even those yuppies whose gentrification of many inner-city
neighborhoods has dislodged thousands of low-income families and
contributed to the current crisis.

5   Estimates of the number of Americans currently without a perma-
nent home vary wildly. Advocacy groups like the National Coalition for
the Homeless say that close to 3 million Americans live on the streets or
in emergency shelters. The U.S. Department of Housing and Urban Development puts the figure at 350,000.

10   Yet the bureaucrats and advocates concur on one point: The face of
homelessness has changed radically in the past 10 years as more and
more low-income housing is mowed down in the name of progress.
Some 20 years ago, says Kristen Morris, assistant director of the New
York office of the National Coalition for the Homeless, the typical "street
15   person" was a White male who suffered from a mental illness or an addiction to drugs or alcohol. Today's homeless are a more eclectic group.

More than 60 percent of the homeless today are Black, mostly
single mothers with small children. More than half of them have never
been homeless before. In many cases, they have been evicted from their
20   homes, or the housing in which they lived was condemned or burned
down. About 60 percent of all homeless people subsist on some form of
public assistance with an average monthly income of $110. About 20
percent are mentally ill. "There's been a real democratization of skid
row," says Maria Foscarinis, an attorney for the Coalition for the Home-
25   less. "All sorts of people have been pushed out of the housing market
because of the critical shortage of affordable places to live."

As a result, homelessness has vaulted to the top of the "me-
generation's" short list of social concerns. But there is a great gulf between concern and active involvement in the effort to remedy this
30   growing problem. For many, the inaction is due to ignorance, not indif-

ference. "There are a lot of people who want to get involved but don't really know how," says Ellen Rocks, executive director of the House of Ruth, a Washington, D.C., organization that provides shelter and other services to women who are homeless or are the victims of domestic
35 violence.

The fact is there are many ways in which individuals can help the homeless. Yet for those truly interested in the cause, one of the first steps, many advocates say, is to get to know the homeless and understand how they became that way. "It's important for middle-class people
40 to reach out to the homeless and bridge the gap that exists," says the Reverend Larry Rice, director of the New Life Evangelistic Center in St. Louis, a group that sponsors programs for the homeless throughout Central Missouri and Illinois. "Middle-class people have to learn that what is happening in America today is all-out war on the poor. Just as
45 America once robbed the Indians of their land, today we're robbing the poor of affordable housing."

The only way to truly get to know the homeless, however, is to work with them in hundreds of shelters and agencies that provide them with assistance. "Most people feel very alienated from the homeless,"
50 says Charles Green, vice president of Partnership for the Homeless. "When they see them on the street, they don't look at them as human beings, they look at them with an attitude of fear, pity or revulsion. But in order to be able to help the homeless, you have to change that outlook. You have to get to know them as people."
55 Working with the homeless can take many forms. Shelters have a groaning need for volunteer staff members to fill a variety of roles. Individuals are needed to help displaced families find affordable housing, to assist homeless persons in their quest for employment, to tutor young mothers studying for high school equivalency exams, and to help chil-
60 dren with their homework. Volunteers are also needed simply to provide emotional support to individuals attempting to climb out of poverty. No talent or skill is too insignificant to be put to use in the fight against homelessness. "When it comes to helping the homeless, there is a lot of work to be done and everybody has something to give," says
65 Sister Lula Walker, director of Chicago's Tabitha House, an agency that provides food, clothing, shelter and job training for homeless women and their children.

For those not inclined or too busy to do volunteer work, there are other ways that they can aid the homeless. Despite the intense media
70 attention focused on homelessness in the past few years, legislators on both the national and local levels have still been slow to respond to the desperate plea for low-income housing. Furthermore, many middle-class communities have adamantly rejected efforts to place scattered low-income units in their neighborhoods, fearing increased crime and
75 lowered property values.

Homeless advocates say that sensitive people are needed to act as emissaries, spreading the message that the housing crisis in this country needs to be addressed. "It's very important for people to get involved in an advocacy campaign," says Marcia Fredericks of Project
80 Unity, a shelter and advocacy group in Los Angeles. "Write to your congressman and city council members to lobby for more affordable housing. Host meetings at your house to discuss the problem with your neighbors and friends. We have to keep this issue before the public and before our representatives in government to break down some of the
85 misconceptions about homelessness and get some things done about it."

Even with more broad-based support, advocates say the problems of the homeless will not be cured overnight. Finding shelter for the destitute, the displaced and the social dropouts will take money and creative solutions. But as more people become involved in the effort, both
90 the money and the solutions become easier to find. "Right now," says Reverend Rice of the New Life Evangelistic Center, "it's like there's this small group of people with their finger in the dike trying to keep the flood of homeless people from spilling over into the street. But with more support, more money, more attention to the needs of the poor, we
95 can build a whole new dam that could save almost anybody."

To find out more about agencies in your area that assist the homeless, write to:

The National Coalition for the Homeless
105 E. 22nd Street
100 New York, NY 10010

From *Ebony Magazine*, vol. 44, no. 8, June 1989.

Check Your Comprehension

1. According to this article, what kinds of changes have there been in the homeless population?

2. According to the different representatives of the homeless, what are the ways that ordinary people can help solve the problem?

3. What did Maria Foscarinis mean when she said, "There's been a real democratization of skid row"?

4. What did Reverend Rice mean when he said, "It's like there's this small group of people with their finger in the dike trying to keep the flood of homeless people from spilling over into the street. But with more support, more money, more attention to the needs of the poor, we can build a whole new dam that could save almost everybody"?

Vocabulary: Paraphrasing

Rewrite the following sentences, paraphrasing the italicized words. You may change other parts of the sentence if you need to, but remember to retain the sentence's original meaning.

1. The *gentrification* of many inner-city neighborhoods has *dislodged* thousands of low-income families.

    _____

    _____

2. A lot of low-income housing has been *mowed down* recently; therefore, the homeless have become a more *eclectic* group.

    _____

    _____

3. Homelessness has *vaulted* to the top of the *short list* of social concerns.

    _____

    _____

4. Shelters for the homeless have a *groaning* need for volunteers to fill a variety of *roles*.

    _____

    _____

5. Many middle-class communities have *adamantly* rejected efforts to place *scattered* low-income units in their neighborhoods.

    _____

    _____

Think About It

1. Why do you think the estimates of the number of homeless people given by different groups vary so much?

2. One suggestion made in this article is to "get to know the homeless." What is the best way to do this? Would you be willing to talk to homeless people?

3. If a homeless person asked you for money, how would you respond?

4. Are there homeless people in your country? How are they treated?

5. Imagine you are a member of the "Committee to Defend the Homeless." The mayor of your city has just announced that, in order to present a better image of the city, all the park benches are going to be replaced with a new type of bench. The new benches are divided into separate seats, so that homeless people cannot sleep on them. How is your committee going to respond? With a group of classmates, prepare a report to the mayor, explaining why you disagree with his proposal. Offer an alternative proposal as well. (You may use the outline given below.)

A REPORT TO THE MAYOR
FROM THE COMMITTEE TO PROTECT THE HOMELESS

A. Problem:

B. Why the benches are unfair:

C. An alternative proposal:

D. Conclusion:

Before You Read

Figure 7.2   House Prices in the Ten Most Expensive U.S. Cities

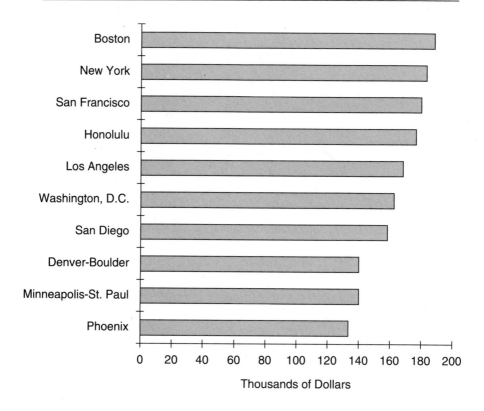

Thousands of Dollars

Source: Bureau of the Census, *Statistical Abstract of the United States, 1989* (Washington, D.C., 1989), table 773.

In the following excerpt, the author went into the subway in New York and found a homeless man to talk to. Here, he tells a little about what it is like to be homeless.

Before you read, think about the following questions:

- Who is responsible for the homeless?
- Do you think homeless people are lazy?

Glossary

Grand Central Terminal Often called *Grand Central Station;* one of the major railroad and subway stations in New York City

Martinique Name of a hotel used as a shelter for the homeless in New York City

Macy's Large department store

Grand Hyatt Large hotel in New York City

Port Authority Public transportation station in New York City

Dante Italian poet (1265–1321) who wrote *The Divine Comedy,* one part of which, "The Inferno," gives a detailed description of Hell

The Bowery Area of New York City, now well known for the number of homeless and transients who stay there

Medicaid Healthcare program for poor and elderly people

About the Author

Jonathan Kozol is the author of the National Book Award-winning *Death at an Early Age* and *Illiterate America.* Over the past 25 years he has been concerned, as a writer and a teacher, with the care and education of children.

Rachel and Her Children
by Jonathan Kozol

Richard Lazarus, an educated, 36-year-old Vietnam veteran I met two days after Thanksgiving in the subway underneath Grand Central Station, tells me he had never been without a job until the recent summer. In July he underwent the loss of job, children, and wife, all in a
5 single stroke. As in almost all these situations, it was the simultaneous occurrence of a number of emergencies, any one of which he might sustain alone, but not all at the same time, that suddenly removed him from his home.

"Always, up until last summer, I have found a job that paid at least
10 $300. Now I couldn't find a job that paid $200. When I found an opening at a department store they said that I was overqualified. If someone had asked me a year ago who are the homeless, I would not have known what to reply. Now I know the answer. They are people like myself. I went to Catholic elementary school. I had my secondary education in a

15 private military school. I joined the service and was sent to Thailand as an airman." He has a trade. It's known as "inventory data processing." He had held a single job in data processing for seven years until last summer when the company shut down, without a warning, and moved out of state.

20   "When the company left I could find nothing. I looked everywhere. I got one job for two months in the summer. Part-time, as a security guard in one of the hotels for homeless families."

When I ask which one it was, he says the Martinique. "I clocked the floors for fire check. From the top floor to the lobby I swore to myself:
25 rat infested, roach infested, drug infested, filth infested, garbage everywhere, and little children playing in the stairs. Innocent people, women, children, boxed in by their misery. Most people are permitted to make more than one mistake. Not when you're poor."

In September he was sick. "I was guarding homeless people and I
30 didn't have a home. I slept in Washington Square and Central Park." He's living now in a run-down hotel operated in conjunction with the Third Street Shelter on the Bowery. "When you come in at night the guards wear gloves. They check you with a metal detector. They're afraid to touch me."

35   While we talk we watch an old man nearby who is standing flat and motionless against the wall, surrounded by two dozen bright-red shopping bags from Macy's. Every so often, someone stops to put a coin into his hand. I notice the care with which the people drop their coins, in order that their hands do not touch his. When I pass that spot some
40 hours later, he will still be there. I'll do the same. I'll look at his hand—the fingers worn and swollen and the nails curled in like claws—and I will drop a quarter and extract my hand and move off quickly.

After standing with Lazarus for two hours before the hot-dog stand, I ask him if he'd like to leave the station to sit down with me and get a
45 decent meal. He's awkward about accepting this. When I press him, he explains he had only one subway token and has no more money. If he leaves the station he will need a dollar to get back inside. He agrees to leave when I assure him I can spare a dollar. Outside on Forty-second Street, we're facing the Grand Hyatt. He looks at it with fear.

50   "The first thing that you see when you come out of there is power."

At a delicatessen next to the Grand Hyatt he explains about the subway tokens. Each morning at the shelter you get in a line in order to receive two subway tokens. This is to enable you to look for jobs; the job search is required. But, in order to get the tokens, you have got to
55 prove that you already have a job appointment. "It's a long line. By the time you get the tokens you have missed the job appointment. You wait

in line for everything. I get the feeling that the point is not to find a job but to teach us something about who we are. Getting us in line is the idea."

60   In the restaurant he orders a chicken sandwich and, although he's nervous and his hands are shaking, he eats fast; he's almost done before I've put a paper napkin in my lap. He apologizes but he tells me that this is the first thing he has had to eat since 8:00 a.m. It's now about 8:30 in the evening.

65   "Before I got into this place I was sleeping in the parks. When it got colder I would sleep all night in an X-rated movie or the subway or the Port Authority. I'd spend most of my time just walking. I would try to bathe each day in public toilets. I'd wash my clothes and lay them outside in the sun to dry. I didn't want to feel like a pariah that nobody
70   would get near. I used to talk with people like yourself so that I would not begin to feel cut off. I invested all my strength in fighting off depression. I was scared that I would fall apart.

"During this time I tried to reunite with my old lady. For me, the loss of work and loss of wife had left me rocking. Then the welfare
75   regulations hit me. I began to feel that I would be reduced to trash. You're never prepared for this. It's like there isn't any bottom. It's not like cracks in a safety net. It's like a black hole sucking you inside. Half the people that I know are suffering from chest infections and sleep deprivation. The lack of sleep leaves you debilitated, shaky. You exag-
80   gerate your fears. If a psychiatrist came along he'd say that I was crazy. But I was an ordinary man. There was nothing wrong with me. I lost my wife. I lost my kids. I lost my home. Now would you say that I was crazy if I told you I was feeling sad?

"I was a pretty stable man. Now I tremble when I meet somebody in
85   the ordinary world. I'm trembling right now. One reason that I didn't want to leave the subway was that I feel safer underground. When you asked if I would come outside and get something to eat, my first thought was that you would see me shaking if we sat down for a meal and you'd think I was an alcoholic.

90   "I've had a bad cold for two weeks. When you're sick there's no way to get better. You cannot sleep in at the shelter. You have got to go outside and show that you are looking for a job. I had asthma as a kid. It was gone for twenty years. Now it's back. I'm always swallowing for air. Before I got into the shelter, I did not have Medicaid or welfare. If you
95   don't have an address it's very hard. I scrambled to get into the computer.

"Asthma's common at the shelter. There's a lot of dust. That may be why. Edema [swollen feet]—you get it from sitting up so much and walking all day long. If you're very hungry and you want a meal you can

get it at St. Francis. You can get a sandwich at Grand Central every
100   night at ten o'clock. So if you want to keep from starving you are always
on the move. If you have no subway tokens then you jump the stile.
You're always breaking rules and so you start to have this sense of pre-
monition: 'Sooner or later I'll be caught.' You live in constant fear.

"A year ago I never thought that somebody like me would end up in
105   a shelter. Nothing you've ever undergone prepares you. You walk into
the place—the smell of sweat and urine hits you like a wall. Unwashed
bodies and the look of absolute despair on many, many faces there
would make you think you were in Dante's Hell. Abandon hope. I read a
lot. I'm not a lazy man.

110   "I slept with my clothes on the first night that I was there. I was
given a cot but they were out of sheets. I lay awake. I heard men crying
in their sleep. They're sound asleep and they are *crying.* What you fear
is that you will be here forever. You do not know if it's ever going to end.
You think to yourself: It is a dream and I will wake. Sometimes I think:
115   It's an experiment. They are watching you to find out how much you can
take. Someone will come someday and say: 'Okay, this guy has suffered
long enough. Now we'll take him back into our world.' Then you wake
up and get in line . . .

"Listen to me: I've always worked. I need to work! I'm not a lazy
120   man." His voice rises and the people at the other tables stare. "If I
thought that I could never work again I'd want to die."

Excerpted from Jonathan Kozol, *Rachel and Her Children: Homeless Families in Amer-*
ica (New York: Fawcett Columbine, 1988).

Check Your Comprehension

1.   What is Richard Lazarus's background? What is his occupation?

2.   What is the irony about Mr. Lazarus working at the Martinique Hotel?

3.   Mr. Lazarus gives two reasons why he doesn't like to come out of
the subway. What are they?

4.   In line 58, Richard Lazarus says, "Getting us in line is the idea."
What does he mean by this?

Vocabulary: Prepositions

Write the correct preposition(s) on the line(s) in each of the following sentences.

1. The benefit dinner was given _____ conjunction _____ a charity auction.

2. You should try to find _____ how to help the homeless.

3. No one enjoys waiting _____ line.

4. If you stay in your room alone, you might begin to feel cut _____ from society.

5. I was invited to two dinner parties, but they were both _____ the same time.

6. I went to visit my old friend, but his landlord said he had moved _____ .

7. His room was so small, he felt boxed _____ .

8. Donna went to bed very late last night, so she is sleeping _____ this morning.

9. Most people don't believe they will ever end _____ homeless.

10. The desk was surrounded _____ a lot of empty boxes.

Think About It

1. According to the article, Mr. Lazarus is educated, has at least seven years of experience in his trade, and wants to work. Why do you think he doesn't have a job?

2. Mr. Lazarus says he never thought he could become homeless—most people don't. Do you think you could ever be homeless? Why or why not?

3. What would you do if you were Mr. Lazarus?

4. How did this reading make you feel? Were you surprised by anything? Saddened? Angry? Explain your answer.

5. Imagine Mr. Lazarus two years from now. What has happened to him? Write a description of the two years, beginning after the author of the reading interviewed him.

PART TWO
Ecology: Blue Skies Above Us

Before You Read

Table 7.1   Polluting Oil and Chemical Spills
in the United States, 1970–1985

	Number of Accidents	Gallons Spilled
1970	3,771	15,253,000
1975	12,781	22,243,000
1980	11,155	15,093,000
1985	11,023	21,718,000

Source: Adapted from U.S. Coast Guard, *Report of the Marine Safety Information System, June 1988.*

People formulate their opinions about the environment from what they hear and what they read. Unfortunately, there is a lot of conflicting information. This reading presents ten "myths" that the author believes people have about the environmental crisis.

Before you read, think about the following questions:

- What do you think is the biggest source of pollution?
- Do you do anything to help improve the environment?

Glossary

Superfund   Government-sponsored and -funded program to clean up severely polluted areas

Love Canal   Area in New York state that was found to be heavily contaminated with toxic waste; all the residents left the area.

Ten Myths About Our Environmental Crisis

by Monte Paulsen

Myth 1: The events at Chernobyl and Valdez were accidents.

The 1986 explosion of a Soviet nuclear reactor and the 1989 ground-
ing of an Exxon oil tanker illustrated the dangers of nuclear- and fossil-
fuel-derived energy. But the dangers had always been there, built into
5 the margin of error inherent in every technology. And these events will
seem petty when the consequences of acid rain and global warming become evident.

Myth 2: Toxic waste comes from industrial pollution.

Workers in yellow rubber suits at Superfund sites like Love Canal
10 make great news pictures, but home cleaning products spread more
toxics. Public awareness of the germ theory of disease, combined with
decades of advertising, led to germ phobia. The big business of household cleaners has translated that into a widespread and unmonitored
source of toxic waste.

15 *Myth 3: Nonbiodegradable products are clogging our landfills.*

Plastic is actually safer than many biodegradable products in a
sealed landfill. The garbage crisis is not caused by what people throw
away. It's caused by how much people throw away—four pounds a day
and rising. The answer is simple and inexpensive: Buy less.

20 *Myth 4: First World countries are opposing the destruction of fragile
Third World environments.*

Third World nations clear land to appease American banks that demand the sort of "development" that will enable those countries to pay
back huge foreign debts. In order to continue receiving money, those
25 countries have no choice but to comply.

Myth 5: Chlorofluorocarbons (CFCs) are the cause of global warming.

Simple carbon dioxide contributes more toward global warming
than do exotic gasses such as CFCs. The average American automobile
pumps its own weight in carbon dioxide into the air each year. And
30 more than 180 million of the 500 million vehicles on Earth are in the
United States, where highway transportation alone accounts for about
27 percent of fossil-fuel-released carbon dioxide.

Myth 6: Water pollution comes from industrial effluent.

35   Since the cleanup efforts of the past two decades, less than 10 percent of water pollutants come directly from industry. Non-point sources, such as oil that drips from automobiles and chemicals that get washed off lawns and fields, account for more than 65 percent of water pollution.

Myth 7: The United States can grow enough food to feed the world.

40   In 1988, U.S. grain production fell below even domestic consumption when farmers who had achieved impressive short-run results by intensive plowing, pumping, and fertilizing were devastated by the drought.

Myth 8: A clean environment is a luxury.

45   Politicians and policy-makers foolishly consider environmental protection a luxury—something to be addressed after economic growth and social welfare are ensured. But in most instances, environmental degradation eventually leads to economic and social degradation.

Myth 9: Birth control programs are needed to stop Third World overpopulation.

50   The Earth's human population of five billion is expected to double during the next century. But birth control alone won't stop overpopulation; the lives of women worldwide must be improved—especially in the "developed" countries, where each child consumes far more energy, raw material, and food than do children in overpopulated nations.

55   *Myth 10: George Bush is an environmentalist.*

During his 1988 campaign, the Texas oilman who led Reagan's anti-regulation crusade made effective use of the polluted waters of Boston Harbor as a campaign issue and told the world, "I am an environmentalist, always have been." But once in office, his administration halved
60   federal funding for sewage treatment facilities, refused to sign a global agreement to ban production of CFCs, and altered scientific testimony to make predictions for global warming appear more uncertain than they were.

From *Casco Bay Weekly* (Maine), Jan. 4, 1990.

Check Your Comprehension

1. Why doesn't the author consider Chernobyl and Valdez "accidents"?
2. How are household chemicals affecting the earth?
3. According to the author, how are Third World countries being pressured to destroy their environments?

Vocabulary: New Terminology

The following words or phrases may not be in the dictionary because they are relatively new. Write detailed definitions for each of them.

1. acid rain
2. global warming
3. toxic waste
4. biodegradable
5. ozone layer
6. fossil fuel

Think About It

1. One underlying message of this article is that ordinary people can improve the environment by changing their lifestyles. What specific things can we do?

2. Do you think any of the author's "myths" are actually facts? Which ones? Why?

3. The environment is a concern in nearly every country on earth. What about your own country? What problems has it faced recently? How is it handling the ecological crisis?

4. With a partner, complete the following survey. Combine your results with those of your classmates.
    a. Do you recycle any of the following items:

        _____ newspaper

        _____ computer paper

        _____ glass bottles

        _____ aluminum cans
    b. Do you use any of the following items:

        _____ plastic cups, plates

        _____ paper plates, cups

        _____ plastic forks, knives and spoons

        _____ disposable diapers
    c. Do you think you waste paper?
    d. Do you turn off any lights you aren't using?
    e. Do you turn off the radio or TV when you aren't listening to it?
    f. Do you drive places you could easily walk to?
    g. Do you use aerosol spray cans?
    h. Do you use a lot of household chemicals, such as insect killer, cleaners, or bleach?

    Discuss your answers with your classmates. Are you willing to change your habits to help save the environment?

Before You Read

Figure 7.3   U.S. Waste Products: Quantity and Type

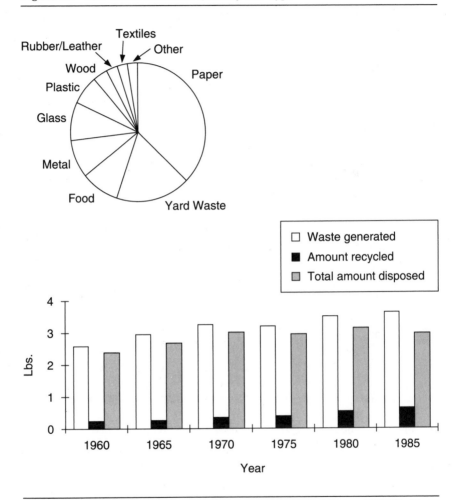

Source: Bureau of the Census, *Statistical Abstract of the United States, 1989* (Washington, D.C., 1989), table 349.

The following reading is taken from an interview with a manager of a salvage yard, or in his words, a "junk man." It provides an interesting look at how one person's garbage can be recycled into another person's treasure.

Before you read, think about the following questions:

- Do you tend to collect things, or would you rather throw things out when you are finished with them?

- How much garbage do you think you throw out during an average day?

Glossary

Styrofoam   Type of artificial material used to make cups and ice chests

Berkeley   City in northern California, near San Francisco

Chevy   Short for Chevrolet, a brand of American automobile

Tales from a Junk Man
by Michael Helm

Managing a salvage yard is a great way to make a living because there is so much waste in this culture. There's tremendous stuff out there, and you winnow through and find something you like. Fifteen years ago, I dropped out of corporate life and got into salvage—actu-
5   ally, it was called junk back then. I wanted to write poetry and have more leisure time. So I bought a pickup truck and started a moving business. In the process of moving people, I hauled their trash away. It amazed me how much of it could still be used and was really worth something.
10   I had truckloads of household items—furniture, music systems, pottery, books. A friend of mine had a garage he wasn't using, and I started storing everything there. When the garage got full, I would have a sale. It was a source of income and a way of recycling, though the word recycling wasn't being used then.
15   Basically what we have now in the cities is a system designed to manufacture garbage. Compactor trucks pick up trash, mix and crush everything, and take it to landfills. If the dumps were to close—if there weren't any place to take trash—probably people would cut their consumption and think twice about what they brought home.
20   As the economy has pinched more and more people, the prejudice against second-hand things has changed. There is a recognition that old things were well made and are durable. Something that is 20 years old is likely to last longer than something made today. I have a '65 Chevy pickup

that is better built than anything you'll find on the road now. I've been
25 driving it for 15 years and probably will be able to drive it another 20.

Even if we started building everything to last, the old things would
still be good and they'd be lower priced because they are old. That's
another aspect of recycling and salvage. There's an egalitarian access,
ultimately, for everybody.

30 My salvage yard in Berkeley, Urban Ore, provides an outlet for
imagination. Once something is second-hand, the whole pattern of advertising is removed from it. Most people are incredibly intimidated to
take something new and use it for a reason other than its original purpose. But once it's second-hand, that goes out the window. If you want
35 to convert a 1957 Chevy convertible into a hot tub, you can.

Certain people who come into the yard are looking for something to
spark their imagination. You can see them eyeing things, trying to discover a new use for something. A lot of it is pretty pedestrian and
foolish, but that's fun, too. Fraternity guys buy cracked used toilets be-
40 cause they just want something to fill with ice and put beer cans in.
They think it's funny. Well, cracked ceramic is better for the ozone
shield than Styrofoam.

Solid core doors can be used as desktops. Clawfoot tubs can hold
goldfish in the back yard. A lot of iron and metal water piping gets used
45 for stakes for terracing gardens. There's an art contingent that comes
into the yard. People will buy a piece of rusted iron because they like
the way it looks. People come in and they'll say, "I'm not into recycling.
I'm just cheap." For them, it's simply rock-hard economics. But a lot of
people combine that bargaining spirit with a sense of ecology, a desire
50 not to exploit the earth.

I assess who the person is and his or her ability to pay. The yuppies
do get soaked a little more because I know they have the money; also,
they're disinclined to bargain as much. The rich don't lower themselves
to haggling about a price.

55 On the other hand, we get people who are barely surviving, probably homeless, and on a rock-bottom level in terms of their ability to survive in a city. For example, you get a guy like Jamie who calls and says
he's got this pedestal sink he wants to bring in. So here's this guy with a
shopping cart that he's borrowed from the Safeway, and he's walking
60 his pedestal sink across town two or three miles to the salvage yard.
When he gets here, it turns out to be this *beige* pedestal sink with good
chunks of enamel broken off and you can see the iron beneath it. It's
something nobody would buy.

There are a lot of people like him who have no money, yet don't
65 want a handout. He wants to give something to get something. He's a
scavenger. Obviously somebody threw that sink out, figuring it was
worthless; he saw it, and he thought, "Ah. Here's a chance for me to

make some money." So I gave the guy five bucks for the effort of doing it, and somehow that all fits into the betterment of the urban scenario.

70   Scavengers are nature's clean-up crew. Things that are lying around have to be taken care of in one way or another. People in the salvage network include everyone from drop-out Ph.D.s to people who got kicked out of school in the seventh grade.

        I dislike the word recycling because it seems so antiseptic. It doesn't
75 have a human element to it. It's too abstract. Conservation is an idea I like as "the right thing to do." But salvage is a process. It's more alive. Salvaging and scavenging include the elements of judgment and discrimination and imagination and freedom. When people ask me what I do, I say, "I run a salvage yard." That feels comfortable to me. It doesn't
80 have any pretension associated with it. I'm not a do-good conservationist. I'm not a pristine recycler. I'm a junk man.

Excerpted from *New Settler*, 1990.

Check Your Comprehension

1. Why did the speaker become a junk man? Why does he like it?
2. Why does the speaker say that the attitude toward used goods has changed?
3. Although the speaker says that Jamie's pedestal sink was worthless, he gave him $5.00 for it. Why?
4. Why does the speaker prefer the description "junk man" to the alternatives?

Vocabulary: Colloquial Language

Complete the following sentences:

1. Second-hand clothing is clothing that has been _____

_____ .

2. The plural of *stuff* is _____; another word for stuff is

_____ .

3. If you think something is junk, you will probably _____

_____ .

4. Another word for a garbage dump is _____

_____ .

5. If you think twice about something, then you _____

_____ .

6. An economy that is pinched is _____

_____ .

7. If you are not into recycling you probably _____

_____ .

8. If the junk man soaks yuppies, he _____

_____ .

9. If you hit rock-bottom financially, you _____

_____ .

10. If a woman gives you a handout, she _____

_____ .

Think About It

1. Do you agree that old things are made better than new things? Why or why not?

2. Do you think that people in your own culture create more or less junk than people in the United States? What specifically is different?

3. What is a garage sale? Have you ever been to one? What do you think about this American custom? Is there anything similar to a garage sale in your own culture?

4. The author explains the uses that some old things can have—doors become desktops; bathtubs become goldfish ponds. Can you think of ways to use the following used items?

   Coffee cups with the handles broken off
   Pens that have run out of ink
   Old tires
   Bathroom sink
   Keys that no longer fit locks
   Lids to jars that have been recycled
   Books in a language you don't read
   Badly scratched record albums

   Think of some other items of "junk" that you could recycle by creating new uses for them.

5. Read the ad (pages 170–171) for the Esprit clothing company, then answer the following questions:
   a. What is unusual about this advertisement?
   b. How is it different from other advertisements you have seen?
   c. Do you think this is an effective way of advertising?
   d. What is the company's purpose in running an ad like this?

A PLEA FOR RESPONSIBLE CONSUMPTION

So often our needs are defined by things that don't get us much the comfort of having lots of stuff, the image we want to portray the social pressure to appear to be affluent, the bizarre idea of having something new for its own sake, like a new car or new TV or the latest fashion. For years, we have spoken to our customers about the difference between fashion and style. We've tried our best to encourage style and reinforce the concept that style isn't a fad. It comes from your imagination and is developed slowly. It's a reflection of your values.

Today, more than ever, the direction of an environmentally conscious style is not to have luxury or conspicuous consumption written all over your attire. This is still our message. We believe this could be best achieved by simply asking yourself before you buy something (from us or any other company) whether this is something you really need. It could be you'll buy more or less from us, *but only what you need*. We'll be happy to adjust our business up or down accordingly, because we'll feel we are then contributing to a healthier attitude about consumption. We know this is heresy in a growth economy, but frankly, if this kind of thinking doesn't catch on quickly, we, like a plague of locusts, will devour all that's left of the planet. We could make the decision to reduce our consumption, or the decision will soon be made *for* us.

We are optimistic that we can change course and avoid the disastrous destination toward which we're heading. We also believe that there are many events occurring throughout the world right now which support this outlook. We've experienced big changes in people's attitudes about some extremely important philosophical issues and values: racial, feminist, and economic systems such as what we're witnessing in Eastern Europe.

Our purchasing habits have enormous influence. By changing the things that make us happy and buying less stuff, we can reduce the horrendous impact we have been placing on the environment. We can buy for vital needs, not frivolous ego-gratifying needs. We do need clothes, yes, but *so many?*

While we're lobbying for responsible consumption, we want to suggest one more idea. What you save, if you do, through changing your purchasing habits, consider contributing to one of the thousands of social and environmental organizations that are working to correct, repair, preserve or halt the damage to which our consumptive ways and economic system have led us.

We all have to work together to preserve the continuity of natural cycles and processes. If we don't, we'll have no inheritance to bestow on our grandchildren. All will be gone. Our place in history will be that of the greatest mismanagers of the Earth, not such a loving way to be remembered!

ESPRIT

A COMPANY THAT IS TRYING

Synthesis

Discussion and Debate

1. The Greek root for the first part of the word *ecology* means 'house.' The meaning has changed through the process of metaphor. Can you see how?

2. Do you think homelessness and the ecological crisis are symptoms of one greater problem, or are they completely independent issues?

3. Some people argue that social problems are the most important problems to solve, while others believe that unless the ecological problems are solved, it will not matter if the social problems are solved. Whom do you agree with? Why?

4. Think of another question to ask your classmates about the ideas presented in this chapter.

Writing Topics

1. What do you think the world's most serious problem is? Write an argument for your opinion, using the outline below:

    The world's most serious problem today is _____

    _____

    _____

    The first reason this is most important is _____

    _____

    _____

    _____

    _____

    The second reason this is most important is _____

    _____

    _____

    _____

    _____

The last reason is _____

_____

_____

_____

_____

In conclusion, _____

_____

_____

_____

_____

2. Now, using the same outline, detail your suggestions for a solution.

The solution to the problem of _____ is

_____

The first way to bring about this solution is _____

_____

_____

_____

_____

The second thing we must do to solve this serious problem is

_____

_____

_____

_____

Finally, we must _____

_____

_____

_____

_____

In conclusion, _____

_____

_____

_____

_____

3. Part of the difficulty with major problems is identifying the person or persons most capable of solving them. For the problem you wrote about in question 1, who do you think is most responsible for bringing about a solution? Write a letter to that person (or people) explaining the nature of the problem, the importance of solving it, and suggestions for the solution. Use the material you wrote for questions 1 and 2 to assist you. (If you wish, mail your letter, and report to the class on the reply.)

On Your Own

1. Find out what volunteer organizations exist to help the homeless or to protect the environment in your area and what specific actions they take to help solve those problems. Report your findings to your classmates.

2. Ask ten U.S.-born Americans what they think the most important problem in the world today is. Compare their answers to your classmates'. Did any of the answers surprise you? Was there one problem that seemed to trouble several people?

3. Sunday television is dedicated to broadcasting serious news and political analysis. Some of the problems you might find on Sunday are *Meet the Press, Face the Nation, 60 Minutes,* and *This Week* with David Brinkley. Check a local television listing and find out what stations carry these shows at what time. Watch one or more of them and report to the class on the political or social problems that were discussed on them.

4. The movies *Ironweed* and *Down and Out in Beverly Hills* deal with the issue of homelessness. Check your video store for one of these movies, and watch it. Review the film for your classmates.

5. Interview someone who works as a volunteer at a homeless shelter or works in an organization whose purpose is to save the environment. Ask this person what his or her role is in the organization and what it is like to participate in that group. Tape record your interview, or take notes and describe the interview to your classmates.

8

Vices:
Habits and
Addictions

PART ONE
Smoking and Drinking: Bottoms Up

Before You Read

Figure 8.1   Percentage of People in the United States Who Smoke, 1970–1985

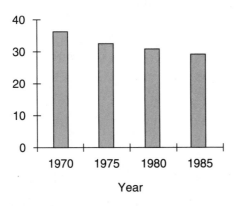

Source: Bureau of the Census, *Statistical Abstract of the United States, 1989* (Washington, D.C., 1989), table 192.

    Smoking tobacco is losing popularity in the United States. As you can see from the figure above, less than 30 percent of the people in the United States smoke now. The author of the following essay discusses how and why he quit smoking.
    Before you read, think about the following questions:

- Do you smoke? If so, would you like to quit?
- What do you think about smoking regulations in the United States?

Glossary

Häagen-Dazs   Popular brand of ice cream

About the Author

Lewis Grizzard is a humor writer from the South who writes about life in the United States.

How I Quit Smoking
by Lewis Grizzard

You can't smoke anymore on New York commuter trains, and it probably won't be very long until you can't smoke anywhere.

You probably can't smoke where you work now, and restaurants and planes are also becoming smoke-free.

5 What happened is the antismokers, obnoxious though they can be, have won, and smokers have become outcasts and subjects of much derision.

If you smoke, there is only one plausible thing left for you to do. You must quit.

10 I know. This comes from a man who smoked his head off for years and loved every cigarette he ever had.

Smoking was one of the great pleasures of my life. A cigarette was like a little reward I gave myself 25 to 40 times a day.

But I quit. For several reasons:

15 • I've already had two heart-valve replacement surgeries and may one day face another. I need to smoke like I need getting poked in the eye with a sharp stick.

• Very few of my friends smoke anymore. I began to feel uncomfortable smoking in front of them.

20 • I fly 150 times a year. Airlines are turning off the smoking lights.

• Flying makes me nervous enough as it is without also craving a cigarette.

• None of my friends believed I really had the courage to stop smoking. I quit to prove them wrong.

25 Here's how I did it, after smoking for twenty-three years:

• I made a pact with three friends that we would stop smoking together.

• I figured at least one of them wouldn't make it and I could start again, too. But they all stayed smokeless and I hung in there 30 with them.

• When the craving was at its worst, I kept telling myself, "Nobody ever died from stopping smoking."

• I also relied on others who quit long ago who said to me, "I know it's hard for you to believe now, but there will come a 35 time you won't even think of a cigarette anymore."

It took me three weeks to reach the point where I actually had a thought other than having a cigarette.

- I substituted eating ice cream for smoking. I put on fifteen quick pounds and made the Häagen-Dazs people rich, but it still
40 helped me quit smoking.

I became an obnoxious nonsmoker myself. I berated a man (a small man) for lighting up in a nonsmoking area of an Amtrak train, and I bragged to friends who continued to smoke after I quit: "Well, all I can say is, I'm glad I'm no longer a slave to tobacco."

45 If I ever start again, I would have to face much finger-pointing and ridicule. That gives me strength to carry on.

I gave myself an out. I'm going to start smoking again on my ninetieth birthday.

Quit, dammit.

From Lewis Grizzard, *Chili Dawgs Always Bark at Night* (New York: Villard Books, 1989), pp. 197–98.

Check Your Comprehension

1. What is the current attitude toward smokers in the United States, according to the author?

2. Now that Grizzard is a nonsmoker, what is his attitude toward smokers?

3. How have the airlines had an influence on the author's decision to quit smoking?

Vocabulary: Word Roots and Meanings

Find the following words in a dictionary that supplies word roots and historical information (the *American Heritage Dictionary* or the *Oxford English Dictionary*, for example). Divide the words into their different meaningful parts, and define each part. (The number after each word indicates the number of parts the word can be divided into.)

1. obnoxious (3)
2. derision (3)
3. plausible (2)
4. pact (1)
5. ridicule (2)

Think About It

1. The author gives many reasons for quitting smoking. What do you think is the best one he gives? Why?

2. The author also gives a list of the things that helped him stop. Which of these do you think probably was the most effective?

3. How is smoking regarded in your own culture?

4. Cigarette companies advertise heavily. Part of their marketing strategy is to give each brand of cigarette an "image" and promote that cigarette to a certain part of the population.

   Find four cigarette advertisements that you think are targeted at different sectors of the population. Identify whom each ad is trying to appeal to and how the ad achieves that purpose.

5. Make a list of all the names of cigarettes you can think of. How does each of these names relate to the image the tobacco company wants to project?

Before You Read

FROZEN MARGARITA

This tart tequila-based specialty, the Margarita, is served in a long-stemmed cocktail glass with a salted rim.

INGREDIENTS:

1.5 ounces tequila
.5 ounce Triple Sec or Cointreau
.5 ounce fresh lime juice
3 ice cubes

Put all the ingredients together in a blender. Blend until the ice is smooth. Rub the rim of the glass with a piece of lime, then dip the rim in salt. Pour the drink into the glass and serve immediately.

The following short story narrates the events of an afternoon after work, particularly the effects of drinking margaritas.

Before you read, think about the following questions:

• Have you ever had a margarita? What did it taste like?

• Do you drink alcohol? If so, what's your favorite drink?

Glossary

The John Hancock   Skyscraper in Chicago

The Windy City   Nickname for Chicago

CBS   Columbia Broadcasting System, a national television network

Lauren Hutton   Famous fashion model and actress

Johnny Carson   Comedian and host (1962–1992) of the very popular television talk show "The Tonight Show," broadcast by the stations of the National Broadcasting Corporation (NBC)

Ali McGraw   Actress well known for her starring role in the film *Love Story*

About the Author

Teresa Yunker was a graduate student at the University of Southern California in Los Angeles when she wrote this story, which was the first she ever had published.

Margaritas

by Teresa Yunker

The Margarita stands tall, beautifully iced, with salt crusted thick around its edges. This margarita is a work of art; this margarita is a gem. Its delicate tint, its proud slice of lime, its promise of tequila bite makes this particular margarita the winner of the evening. Of course it
5 is the first margarita. That one is always the finest.

She reaches for it.

"Wait a minute," he says. "A toast to, well, to . . ."

"To us," she says, not caring that it is hardly original. They click glasses and have their first sip. She smiles at him and he smiles back. It
10 is Thursday evening. They have met here right after work. They work in the same building, the John Hancock. She works for an advertising agency, he works for a law firm. Right now they are in a place called El Jardín, which means The Garden. El Jardín is known for its dangerous margaritas. Otherwise the food is Chicago Mexican rather than Califor-
15 nia Mexican. The waiter appears.

"Do you want anything to eat? Some guacamole?"

"No, this is fine for now."

They are sitting outside on the patio. The weather has not yet
turned cold even though it is October. Of course she doesn't want any-
20 thing to eat. Ruin this first margarita?

"Well," he says, putting down his margarita and inching his chair
closer. "Now I can find out more about you."

"And spoil the mystery?" she says. My god, what a line.

"So how do you like Chicago so far?"

25   "Fine, just fine."

It seems he had seen her driving to work in a car with California
plates. She hadn't learned then that it was easier to use the subways.

"You prepared for winter?"

"Hardly!" And they laugh as if she's said something hilarious. They
30 both take deep swallows from their drinks. Her mouth feels particularly
sharp from the salt. "Really, I can't imagine it," she says. "Thirty below
and all that."

"Well, you'll find out. This isn't called the Windy City for nothing.
Sure isn't California!"

35   Yes, well. She hopes to get him off the California bit.

"So you're a lawyer?"

"Working on it. Right now I'm in law school and working part-time
at a law firm."

"Uh-huh."

40   "What do you do at the advertising agency?"

"Well, just about everything." Her margarita is nearly finished. She
glances around for the waiter.

"You know, it's hard for me to have any time at all between law
school and work. Law school is really something . . . the time it eats
45 away." Ah, she sees, he wants to talk about himself but that's okay because the second margarita is placed before her, all fresh and clean.

"It must be very difficult."

"Oh, it is," he says, leaning forward. "I hardly have time for anything other than classes, studying, and work. It's been hard to meet
50 people."

"I can imagine."

By people she supposes he means women. Here he is with her on
what is probably his first date in months.

"Law students are all so uptight, you know? Including me I guess,
55 but you can't study all the time, right?"

"Right."

He has hardly touched his margarita. She had better go slower.

"Conservatism is what you would call it. Do you call yourself conservative?" She is bemused. Exactly what does he mean, conservative?
60 "I mean, the Midwest must be very different than California that way."

"Well, yes, in a way."

"And you're an artist, too. I noticed your way of dressing right away. I could tell you were an artist."

"I'm certainly flattered, being called an artist," she says, "but com-
65 mercial art is bound by certain, uh, certain . . ." What was she saying? Is this a serious conversation?

"I mean, certainly it's more creative than law, say."

"I don't know anything about law . . ."

"You have to come up with ideas and everything, right? I'll have to
70 start watching TV more carefully."

"Oh, I don't do anything for television . . ."

"The colors, the makeup, the actors . . ."

"No, I do ads for mag—"

"Did you work for CBS or something in California?"

75 Her head is spinning. What are they talking about? She sips her drink to clear her head.

"I know it's a typical thing to ask, you know, like have you met any of the stars. Of course you must get asked that all the time really, except you did work for TV out there and people just naturally assume,
80 you know . . ."

"No, I never . . ."

". . . at least people like that, maybe in a restaurant or something, but it's a stupid thing to ask, really but maybe you did meet a model, Lauren Hutton, say . . ." He takes a gulp of margarita. Is she right? Is he
85 asking her if she's ever met Lauren Hutton? Lauren Hutton! "It must have been really interesting to work in TV," he concludes.

"So have you ever . . . well, I was wondering . . ."

There is still margarita left, but hardly any salt. It needs salt. "Oh yes, lots. You'd be surprised how many big-time stars want to be in com-
90 mercials. So lucrative, really." She'd had a little trouble over the word *lucrative*. But he doesn't notice. He is glowing.

"I bet! I bet it's lucrative! Yessir!"

Really, the last bit in the glass just isn't any good without the salt. It's all ice, anyway. Just melted ice. Anyone could see that.

95 "Imagine all that money!" he says. He looks a bit damp in his suit.

"You should take off your tie," she tells him.

"Damn right it's lucrative!" he says. "Hey, time for another, wouldn't you say? Hey, waiter!"

"You really should take off that tie."

100 "My tie?"

"You look really hot." He seems confused. He looks as if he's forgot-
ten where he is. Maybe he has.

"Well, sure, if you say so. Why the hell not? I'm not at work now, am I? So why the hell am I wearing this tie? I'll take it off right now!" He

105   grabs it and yanks it so violently that the table shakes. "So how about those margaritas, huh?" She sees the waiter bearing down on them with his tray of drinks.

"Here they come," she says, but he doesn't seem to hear.

"Didn't we order them awhile ago?" he asks. "So where are they?"

110   He snaps his fingers, his elbow nearly smashing into the tray. The waiter backs off. "Ah, here they are!" he says. "Here's our margaritas! Say, you want something to eat? Some nachos or something?"

The waiter sets down her third margarita, all shining with salt.

"I'm not hungry."

115   "Fine! Later, we'll eat later," and he gestures hugely with one hand.

Hmmm. It just tastes better and better. She'll have to come here again. What's the name? El, El, well of course they all begin with El. Or La. She starts to giggle.

"What's so funny? Huh? What are you laughing at? You laughing at

120   me?" He is grinning wildly at her. Around his forehead bits of damp hair are sticking up like porcupine quills. He keeps raking his head.

"I was just thinking of the time I saw Johnny Carson fall on his ass," she says.

"You are kidding me! Carson on his ass! That's terrific!"

125   "He, he," she gasps for breath between snorts, "he tripped right over my foot and fell backwards on his ass!"

"Tripped over your foot?"

"That's right, and then he leaped up like nothing happened and apologized for stepping on my shoe!"

130   "That is wild! Did this happen at work? At CBS?" He just seems enormous to her suddenly, all sweaty with huge, glazed eyes.

"Oh no, this was at the Christmas party."

This is amazing. Carson and the Christmas party? Well, why not? Why not put some glamour into this poor guy's life? "Every year at

135   Christmas there's this big party and all the stars come and kiss ass because they want to do commercials for us."

His mouth drops open. "Like who?"

"Well, like, like, uh, Ali McGraw, say." How in God's name did she come up with Ali McGraw? "If the truth were to be told I don't give a

140   damn about Ali McGraw." He just gapes at her. "That's right. Who the hell is she? Just some actress, right?"

"Do they have sex at these parties?"

"You know," she says to him, "you shouldn't care so much about these people." This statement moves her deeply. He should listen to her.

145   She is telling him something important. Something that could change his life. She takes a long drink. He is staring at her blindly.

"Do they?"

"Huh?" She hasn't followed, that much is clear. He wants something.

She turns her head away and the potted plants sway sickeningly.
150 The tinny, Mexican music seems very loud. "Did you just ask . . ." she
begins. It is so loud out here. They are outside, aren't they? "Are we still
here?" she asks. "Are we outside still?"

He is getting impatient. He is tapping the tabletop with emphasis on
each beat. He has long thin fingers and she is suddenly convinced he'll
155 make a fantastic lawyer.

"So, what, are you trying to tell me they don't? 'Cause I know for a
fact that they do. Everybody knows that. Those people are so rich,
they'd do anything for excitement. Life must get bloody dull when
you're so rich you can go anywhere. Imagine that! I hear a lot of them
160 are gay. Lots of actors are, you know. Right? So what happens? Tell
me!" He looks right at her. She is scared of him.

"Well, I don't really know . . ."

"But you were there! You just said Carson fell over your foot! Was
he on something? Was that it?"
165   Is this really happening?

"It was just a joke," she says, "I was kidding you."

"I bet he was high. I bet it was coke. You do coke? But what am I
saying, of course you do, you're in TV. I've done it now and then, but it's
so expensive. But that's not *their* problem, right? You want another?"
170   "Oh no, thanks."

"And you too, huh? Of course you must join in on all of this. Maybe
in a way so as not to lose your job or anything, right?"

She chokes on her drink.

"Being a commercial artist and a Hollywood starlet are two differ-
175 ent things. Besides, it's the 1980s, not the 1950s." She isn't sure what she
means by this, but it stops him temporarily.

"Now come on," he says after a minute. "You mean to say that you
don't sleep around at those things? You mean to tell me that?"

"I don't have to tell you anything!"
180   He looks at her like he can't believe his ears. "Hey now, you listen to
me. You started this, you know. You brought up all this crap about Carson. So now I want to hear it."

She was sick with anger. She downs the last of her margarita.

"Will you order me another, honey?" she says, standing up. She
185 can't believe her own voice. It's as sweet as chocolate.

"Where are you going?" His expression is still sullen, but a smile is
beginning. He has taken in the *honey.*

"Just to the bathroom. Be right back." And she waggles her fingers
at him. She has to concentrate hard not to list from side to side. It takes
190 a bit to find the door but once out onto the street, the walk to the subway doesn't seem too long.

The next day at work she is in the elevator before she sees him standing in the back. She curses to herself as the doors close.

"Hi there!" he says, his cheerful voice rising from the rear. Her head
195 cracks.

"Hello," she calls, without turning around. The people in the elevator shuffle with irritation.

"Cold enough for you?"

"Certainly is."

200 This morning, abruptly, it has turned cold. She is in Chicago—angry, capricious Chicago.

"Might snow soon, you know. What do you think of that?" he continues.

"Wow," she says and like a blessing the door opens at her floor. She
205 walks out.

"See you, California." There is special emphasis on the word *California*. She whips around with a wide, dazzling smile.

From John Miller, ed., *Hot Type* (New York: Collier/Macmillan, 1988).

Check Your Comprehension

1. What is the conversation like at the beginning of this story? When and why does it begin to change? How can you tell that the characters are becoming intoxicated?

2. What does the woman do for a living? What does the man think she does?

3. Why does the woman lie to her date about the movie stars that she met?

4. What is the young man's stereotype of California?

Vocabulary: Colloquial Language

The conversation and the woman's thoughts in this story reflect the informal way in which many people speak. What do the following phrases mean, and how might you say them in a simpler, more direct form?

1. "Really, I can't imagine it. Thirty below and all that."

_____

2. "This isn't called the Windy City for nothing."

_____

3. She hopes to get him off the California bit.

_____

4. "Law school is really something."

_____

5. "Law students are all so uptight, you know?"

_____

6. "I bet it's lucrative! Yessir!"

_____

7. "If the truth were to be told I don't give a damn about Ali McGraw."

_____

8. "Was he on something? Was that it?"

_____

Think About It

1. Toward the end of the story, the people on the elevator are irritated with the conversation of the two main characters. Why do you think they are annoyed? What other elevator behavior have you noticed in the United States? Is it different from the elevator behavior in your culture?

2. In the very last line of the story, although the woman has been annoyed by the young law student, she smiles when he calls her "California." Why do you think she smiles?

3. The legal drinking age throughout most of the United States is 21. What is the drinking age in your country? Do you think the legal drinking age in the United States is too high?

4. One problem associated with alcohol consumption is the people who drive while they are drunk. Thousands of people every year are injured or killed by drunk drivers. Create a public service announcement (PSA)—a type of commercial—that tells people why they should not drink and drive. Your PSA should be one minute long.

PART TWO
Drugs: Going Haywire

Before You Read

Figure 8.2   Drug Arrests and Convictions in the United States, 1984–1987

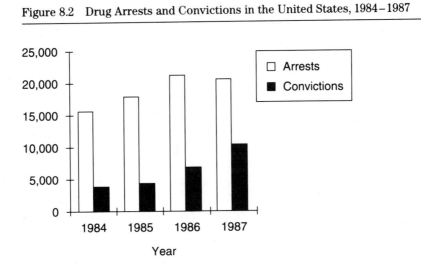

Source: Adapted from U.S. Drug Enforcement Agency, *Annual Statistical Report* (Washington, D.C., 1988).

Drugs are a serious problem in the United States, but different suggestions for solving the problem have become a topic of debate. In this interview, a leading advocate of drug legalization explains the reasons why he believes in legalizing drugs and how to do it successfully.

Since this is an interview, the dialogue alternates between the reporter for the magazine *Mother Jones*, abbreviated "MJ" and Professor Nadelmann, whose name is abbreviated "N." The interviewer's first two questions are hypothetical.

Before you read, think about the following questions:

- Are drugs legal or illegal in your country?
- Are you in favor of legalizing drugs in the United States?

Glossary

George Shultz   Former secretary of state under Republican president Ronald Reagan

William Bennett   Former secretary of education under Republican president Reagan; later "Drug Czar," or overseer of drug programs, in the United States under President George Bush

Milton Friedman   Well-known economist

William Buckley   Conservative spokesman and writer

THC   Chemical found in marijuana

PCP   Type of animal tranquilizer, used illegally by some people as a drug

crack   Very powerful smokable form of cocaine

Riker's Island   New York prison

Phoenix House   Drug treatment center

Head Start Program   Preschool program for young children whose families are poor; it was created to help prepare children for school.

About the Author

Emily Yoffe is a writer who contributes to several popular magazines.

How to Legalize
by Emily Yoffe

Princeton professor Ethan Nadelmann has been one of the earliest and most listened to voices in favor of drug legalization. His argument that the most violent, outlaw economies created by drug prohibition are worse than drug use itself has attracted some strange
5 *bedfellows lately: George Shultz, Milton Friedman, and William F. Buckley. Suddenly the political dividing line seems to be shifting from* <u>should</u> *drugs be legalized to* <u>how</u>*? Here is where the free marketeers on the Right clearly part ways with Dr. Nadelmann.*

MJ: **Drug czar William Bennett is out and you're in. What's the**
10 **first thing you do?**

NADELMANN: The case for legalizing marijuana is an extremely powerful one. But my idea of legalization is not based on the tobacco model, in which we make a highly addictive and deadly substance available at seven cents apiece to be sold in vending machines in packages of
15 twenty. What you do is make it available, more or less like alcohol is made available, in places where it is relatively controlled, where you have to show proof of ID. With legal marijuana you could have the THC content and health warnings on the label.

But one thing we can't afford is to have tobacco companies come to
20 dominate the marijuana business. We can't afford to have pharmaceutical companies come to dominate the cocaine business. Talk about pushing. Look at the tobacco industry internationally. Do they ever make an effort not to have it sold to children? Look at alcohol advertising. That's pushing. They outdo drug dealers any day of the week. I'd
25 like to see the federal tax on tobacco and alcohol doubled or tripled. That would significantly reduce consumption, especially among new users, but would not raise the price so high it would encourage a black market.

MJ: So marijuana is legal—what next?
30 N: On a realistic level, we're going to have to go step by step. For example, legalizing marijuana is not going to change the situation in the inner cities. We have to do with economics what we know we can't do with law enforcement. Let's say we decide, okay, we're not going to legalize crack; what we will do is legalize 15-percent cocaine. About ten
35 years ago the average potency of cocaine on the street was 12 percent. Last year it was about 60 percent, and is going higher. When people said in the seventies that cocaine wasn't that dangerous, maybe that's because it was a lot less potent. So let's say the government will make available 15-percent-pure cocaine. What would happen? Clearly a lot of
40 people using 60-percent cocaine would be just as satisfied with 15 percent. They would be better off, in all likelihood, because they are using a weaker drug and not as much of it.

Yes, some people are still going to want to go to the black market and buy from people who are cooking up the 15-percent cocaine into
45 crack. You won't be able to prevent that. But let's say 70 percent of the market will be using the legal, less potent substance. That's good, because the government taxes it, regulates it, because people know what they're getting. The government has no control right now.

MJ: What would you do about PCP, methamphetamine, heroin?
50 N: I don't think it's a good idea to introduce particular types of drugs into places where there is no demand for them. If there is no market for PCP in Cleveland, I don't think the government should make it available there. But if there is a lot of PCP use in Washington, then the government comes in and regulates its sale. The object is to undercut the
55 criminal element.

MJ: **In most of our cities there are six-month waiting lists for publicly funded drug treatment programs. . . .**

N: It's one of the great hypocrisies of our policies. Drug treatment often turns out to have a lower recidivism rate than throwing people in prison. It's also a lot cheaper. It costs $52,000 a year to keep someone on Riker's Island. A year's stay at Phoenix House in New York, for example, costs about $15,000. The problem is, treatment sounds like a "liberal" solution. Politicians want to sound like they're tough on drugs. If something works better, but it doesn't sound tough, they can be hurt for advocating it.

Everything we know about addiction shows that people who come from stable, supportive environments, who have positive things going for them, have very low rates of addiction. You take people with none of those things, and exactly the same substances lead to much higher rates of addiction.

MJ: **Then isn't that an argument *against* legalization? Shouldn't we be trying to protect the most vulnerable in our society? Why add another problem?**

N: That's exactly the reason *for* legalization. Because criminalization has totally failed to keep crack and other drugs out of the ghetto so far, and offers no promise to do so in the future. Legalization would help eliminate the worst effects of drugs on the community—the rising violence, rising crime, little kids growing up with drug dealers as role models.

Right now the best and the brightest of the ghetto kids understand the economic incentive of drug dealing. It's the drug dealers who have the fancy cars, wads of money, beautiful women. Imagine that instead you have a government-licensed crack outlet, where crackheads line up each day to get their fix. Which is going to send the message you want to send? It seems to me it's better for kids to see the addicts lining up at the crack outlet than to see how cool it is to be a guy who's selling drugs.

In the ghettos it's understandable why people want to obliterate reality. We can't stop drug use until we address the underlying problems in the ghettos. That means, at least in part, more pre- and post-natal programs, more Head Start programs—things that make a difference. But in the meantime, we can at least get rid of the screwed-up incentives our current drug policies provide.

MJ: **What do you see when you look into the future of the drug situation?**

N: You hear knowledgeable people in pharmaceutics and biochemistry say that the knowledge to manufacture mind-altering substances at home is the type of knowledge anybody with a high school chemistry

100 education will have. What are we going to do then—ban high school chemistry courses? In ten or fifteen years, criminal measures may well be totally irrelevant; they won't have a hope of controlling drug use.

Almost every society that we know of in human history has found some form of chemical substance to alter one's state of consciousness. Some societies have been very successful at integrating this into their
105 culture and using it in almost totally nondestructive ways. Somehow public policy has to find a way of encouraging people not to abuse drugs, or at least to use them more safely. Then we need to find the best ways to deal with those people who don't know how to use them safely. Not by throwing them in jail, but by finding ways to help them.

From *Mother Jones*, Feb./March 1990.

Check Your Comprehension

1. Why doesn't Nadelmann think the tobacco or alcohol companies should be involved in the legal drug business?

2. Why would cocaine users be "better off" with government controlled cocaine, according to Nadelmann?

3. Why does Nadelmann think that politicians don't advocate drug treatment?

4. What are some of the problems in the ghetto, according to Nadelmann, and why is eliminating drugs going to be difficult there?

Vocabulary: New Words

Fill in the blanks in the sentences below with one of the following words. Use each word only once. You may need to change the form of the word.

prohibition   legalize   addictive
pharmaceutical   hypocrisy   incentive
obliterate   vulnerable

1. Crack cocaine is highly _____.

2. The _____ industry is responsible for manufacturing legal drugs.

3. Many people claim that the _____ of alcohol was a failure, since many people drank anyway.

4. More and more social critics think that drugs should be

    _____ .

5. Some teenagers find _____ in the fact that their
    parents smoke cigarettes, but won't allow them to.

6. Many addicts need a powerful _____ to stop using
    drugs.

7. It is the goal of the U.S. government to _____ all
    illegal drugs.

8. Children are particularly _____ to the effects of
    narcotics.

Think About It

1. Do you agree with Dr. Nadelmann, or do you believe that drugs
    should remain illegal? Why?

2. Dr. Nadelmann states at the end of this interview that some societies
    have been successful in integrating drug use into their cultures in
    nondestructive ways. Do you know of any of these cultures?

3. Are drugs a problem in your culture? How are drug users handled
    by the government?

4. The drug problem looks different to different people. Dr. Nadelmann
    is a university professor, so some might say he is very "intellectual"
    but that his argument is not based on reality. Look at the list of
    people given below, and try to think of how each person might see
    the drug problem.
    a. A police officer who works in the ghetto
    b. A doctor who works in a hospital emergency room
    c. A casual user of marijuana
    d. The mother (or father) of a boy who has died from a heroin
       overdose
    Now, assume the role of one of these characters. With a partner,
    prepare an interview similar to the one you have just read—your
    partner will ask you about your opinions on drug legalization. You
    will answer as your character. Then switch roles.

Before You Read

Table 8.1   Drug Use by Age Group in the United States, 1985

	Age					
	12–17		18–25		26 and Over	
Drug	% Ever Used	% Now Use	% Ever Used	% Now Use	% Ever Used	% Now Use
Marijuana	23.7	12.3	60.5	21.9	27.2	6.2
Hallucinogens	3.2	1.1	11.5	1.6	6.2	***
Cocaine	5.2	1.8	25.2	7.7	9.5	2.1
Heroin	***	***	11.4	2.1	5.6	.9
Stimulants	5.5	1.8	17.3	4.0	7.9	.7
Alcohol	55.9	31.5	92.8	71.5	89.3	60.7
Cigarettes	45.3	15.6	76.0	37.2	80.5	32.8

*** = less than .5%
Source: Adapted from U.S. National Institute on Drug Abuse, *National Household Survey on Drug Abuse* (Washington, D.C., 1986) (Population estimates, 1985).

The following account describes what it is like to be addicted to heroin, and what the author did to get rid of his addiction.

Before you read, think about the following questions:

- What kind of people do you think become heroin addicts?
- Why do you think people use drugs?

Glossary

junk   Slang for *heroin*

Tangier   City in the country of Morocco, not far from the southern tip of Spain

Scottish terrier   Type of small dog

About the Author

William S. Burroughs is a novelist who was born in St. Louis, Missouri, in 1914. He received his undergraduate degree from Harvard. He was a heroin addict for thirteen years and wrote *Naked Lunch* in 1959, which tells of some of his experiences with addiction.

Kicking Drugs: A Very Personal Story
by William S. Burroughs

I was on junk for almost fifteen years. In that time I took ten cures. I have been to Lexington and have taken the reduction treatment. I have taken abrupt withdrawal treatments and prolonged withdrawal treatments; cortisone, tranquilizers, antihistamines and the prolonged sleep cure. In every case I relapsed at the first opportunity.

Why do addicts voluntarily take a cure and then relapse? I think on a deep biological level most addicts want to be cured.

Junk *is* death and your body knows it. I relapsed because I was never physiologically cured until 1957. Then I took the apomorphine treatment under the care of a British physician, the late Dr. John Yerbury Dent. Apomorphine is the only agent I know that evicts the "addict personality," an old friend who used to inhabit my body. I called him Opium Jones. We were mighty close in Tangier in 1957, shooting 15 grains of methadone every hour, which equals 30 grains of morphine and that's a lot of junk. I never changed my clothes. Jones likes his clothes to season in stale rooming-house flesh until you can tell by a hat on the table, a coat hung over a chair, that Jones lives there. I never took a bath. Old Jones don't like the feel of water on his skin. I spent whole days looking at the end of my shoe just communing with Jones.

Then one day I saw that Jones was not a real friend, that our interests were in fact divergent. So I took a plane to London and found Dr. Dent, with a charcoal fire in the grate, Scottish terrier, cup of tea. He told me about the treatment and I entered the nursing home the following day. It was one of those four-story buildings on Cromwell Road; my room with rose wallpaper was on the third floor. I had a day nurse and a night nurse and received an injection of apomorphine—one twentieth grain—every two hours.

Now every addict has his special symptom, the one that hits him hardest when his junk is cut off. Listen to the old-timers in Lexington talking:

"Now with me it's puking is the worst."

"I never puke. It's this cold burn on my skin drives me up the wall."

"My trouble is sneezing."

With me it's feeling the slow painful death of Mr. Jones. I feel myself encased in his old gray corpse. Not another person in this world I want to see. Not a thing I want to do except revive Mr. Jones.

The third day with my cup of tea at dawn the calm miracle of apomorphine began. I was learning to live without Jones, reading newspapers, writing letters (usually I can't write a letter for a month), and
40 looking forward to a talk with Dr. Dent who isn't Jones at all.

Apomorphine had taken care of my special symptom. After ten days
I left the hospital. During the entire cure I had received only two grains
of morphine, that is, less than I had been using in one shot. I went back
to Tangier, where junk was readily available at that time. I didn't have
45 to use will power, whatever that is. I just didn't want any junk. The apomorphine treatment had given me a long calm look at all the gray junk
yesterdays, a long calm look at Mr. Jones standing there in his shabby
black suit and gray felt hat with his stale rooming-house flesh and cold
undersea eyes.

From *Harper's Magazine*, July 1967.

Check Your Comprehension

1. Who is "Opium Jones"? What is he like?

2. What does Burroughs mean when he says that every addict has "his
    special symptom"? What is his?

3. What do you think Lexington (line 29) is?

Vocabulary: Definitions

Find five words in this account that you didn't know before you read it.
Write each word, and then write a sentence using it.

1. _____ , _____
    _____

2. _____ , _____
    _____

3. _____ , _____
    _____

4. _____ , _____
    _____

5. _____ , _____
    _____

Think About It

1. Why do you think Burroughs wrote this article?

2. Do you think that Burroughs would agree with the idea that drugs should be made legal?

3. What is the difference between *physiological* addiction and *psychological* addiction? How is this difference related to Burroughs' story?

4. Imagine that you are "Opium Jones." Finish the following conversation between William S. Burroughs and yourself.

   BURROUGHS: I am sorry, Mr. Jones, but you will have to leave.
   JONES: Why? I thought we were friends.
   BURROUGHS:

Synthesis

Discussion and Debate

1. Many people argue that beer and alcohol advertising should be made illegal. Do you agree? Do you think it would have any effect on consumer behavior? If drugs are made legal, should they be advertised as well?

2. Many different factors contribute to people's abusing drugs, alcohol, and other substances. What do you think is the most important cause of substance abuse?

3. There have been several court cases in which a tobacco or alcohol company has been sued by the family of a person who died from using the product. Do you think that these companies have any responsibility to the people who are harmed by their products? Why or why not?

4. Think of another question to ask your classmates about the material presented in this chapter.

Writing Topics

1. Do you have an "addiction"? To beer, pizza, ice cream, video games, or something else? Write one paragraph describing your addiction, and then another paragraph explaining a method to cure it. (If you don't have an addiction, invent one.)

2. Imagine that drugs have been legalized in the United States. Write a description of the changes that have taken place because of their legalization.

3. Although drug use is generally recognized as one of the greatest problems in the United States, some might disagree. Look at the following statistics:

Annual Deaths from Substance Abuse

Tobacco — 346,000
Alcohol — 125,000
Alcohol and Drugs — 4,000
Heroin/Morphine — 4,000
Cocaine — 2,000
Marijuana — 75

Source: "Learning and Unlearning Drug Abuse in the Real World," *Research 84* (1988)

Use the arguments you have read in this chapter and the statistics that have been presented to write a short essay explaining what you think is the biggest substance abuse problem in the United States.

On Your Own

1. The following films deal with drug addiction or alcohol:

    Clean and Sober   *Arthur*   *Cocaine Blues*
    The Lost Weekend   *The Days of Wine and Roses*

    Borrow any of them from your local video rental library and give a review of the film you saw to your class.

2. Ask ten U.S.-born Americans the following questions. Report your results to the class.
    a. Do you think drugs should be legalized? (If so, which ones?)
    b. Do you think that a drinking age of 21 is fair?
    c. Do you think cigarette advertising should be banned?
    d. Do you think alcohol advertising should be banned?

3. Look through some magazines and newspapers for "anti" advertising—that is, antidrug, antismoking, and antialcohol messages. Which of them do you think are effective? Why? Which are not? Why not?

4. The game below has many different names, but it is most simply
    called "Categories." The purpose is to fill each square of the game
    with the name of an item that both fits the category and begins with
    a particular letter of the alphabet. How many of the squares can
    you fill? (One has been done for you. Don't despair if you can't get
    them all!)

Category   Begins with the letter . . .

	M	A	C	S
The name of a cocktail	*Margarita*			
The brand name of a beer				
The brand name of a type of cigarette				
A type of alcohol				
A type of drug				

Entertainment:
No Business Like
Show Business

PART ONE
Television: The Boob Tube

Before You Read

Table 9.1 TV Facts

---

*Total hours of television watched in American households in a year: about 231 billion.

*Percentage of Americans who get all of their information about the world from television: 70.

*Percentage of Americans who say they do not watch TV: 8.

*Number of murders the average child has seen on television by the age of sixteen: 18,000.

*Number of commercials American children see by age eighteen: 350,000.

*Number of children born every day: 250,000; number of TV sets made every day: 250,000.

*Number of television sets in 1947: 170,000; in 1948: 250,000; today: more than 750 million.

*Chances that an American has been on television: 1 in 4.

*Percentage of Americans who think commercials are a fair price for free TV: 72.

*Average program time between commercials in the United States: 9.5 minutes.

Source: From "TV Facts," *Connoisseur*, Sept. 1989.

    This reading concerns the phenomenon known as "Couch Potatoes," people whose primary entertainment is sitting on the sofa watching television. The author explains why this form of entertainment is growing in popularity.

    Before you read, think about the following questions:

- How much television do you watch each day?
- Why do you think people watch so much television?

Glossary

baby boom Generation of children born immediately after World War II, continuing to 1960; *boom* refers to the large numbers of babies that were born during that time.

LSD Type of hallucinogenic drug popular in the 1960s

youthquake Word made by combining *youth* and *quake* (from *earthquake*); it suggests that the influence of the young on U.S. society in the 1960s was like that of an earthquake.

Gallup Poll Organization that conducts surveys of the American public about their opinions and behaviors

Arbitron Another national polling organization; most of the surveys it conducts concern the media.

Couch Potatoes: The New Nightlife
by David Blum

The Couch Potato phenomenon is the result of three increasingly important facts of baby-boom life: marriage, children, and home video (not necessarily in that order). Of course, every generation has its own natural ebb and flow of social activity. But in the last twenty years,
5 drugs like cocaine provided the stamina for late-night life, and hallucinogens like LSD and marijuana made the world beyond apartments seem that much more exciting and different. Rock music and pop culture took off in a late-night direction, with discos and night-clubs open till morning for those who could never get enough. And those who were
10 a part of the sixties "youthquake" have been especially resistant to the notion of growing up. Now they're doing it with a vengeance.

"We see it everywhere. People don't want to go out anymore; they'd rather stay in their living rooms," says Keith McNally, the 35-year-old co-owner of Nell's. "And fortunately, we made our club look as much
15 like a living room as we possibly could. Frankly, I'm not the type that likes to go to discos and nightclubs; I'd rather stay home and listen to an album. And that seems to go for almost everybody."

A recent Gallup Poll bears out the stay-at-home theory. In an April 1986 survey that asked the question "What is your favorite way of
20 spending an evening?" one third of all Americans chose the TV set as the preferred means of entertainment. The number of people who gave "resting, relaxing" as their favorite activity—which a Gallup spokeswoman said includes sleeping or stretching out on the sofa—had nearly doubled since 1974, to 14 percent.

25   As one might expect, sociologists take the stay-at-home trend seriously.

"The need to stay at home begins with a change in lifestyle, and of course marriage and children contribute to that in this generation," says Eviatar Zerubavel, a sociologist at the State University of New York at Stony Brook who has studied how people use their time. But he believes that part of the trend is a basic change in attitude toward the home itself.

"What we are really seeing," says Zerubavel, "is a reaction to bureaucratization, and a redefinition of privatization. As people use computers at home instead of working in offices, they will lose their sense of boundaries and the home will represent something less private. Instead of going to bars or the town square, they will be able to meet people via their computer terminals. And that will lead to a lack of desire to lead a public life."

40   There is no way to prove that the number of Couch Potatoes has increased, but the National Center for Health Statistics documents the widely held notion that more people are getting married later and having children later—which is the most important motivational force behind the trend. In 1963, the center's studies put the median age for marriage at 21 for women and 24 for men; by 1984, the median number had climbed to 23 for women and 27 for men.

And children have followed. In 1984, the last year for which the center has figures, women 30 and over gave birth to 882,205 babies, a 69 percent increase over a decade earlier, when women in that age group had only 520,611 babies.

But while every generation gets married and has kids, one technological innovation has made this generation more supine than ever: the videocassette recorder, the magic machine of the new Couch Potato.

VCRs have come close to overtaking all forms of live, outside-the-house entertainment. In 1986, the number of videocassettes rented (1 billion) matched the number of movie tickets that were sold. Close to 45 million homes now have VCRs—more than half the nation's TV households. An Arbitron survey last November showed that in New York City, roughly 3 million households, or 44 percent, owned a VCR.

60   The growth has taken place largely over the last five years: In 1981, Americans spent only $141.8 million on videocassette rentals, and by 1985, that figure had grown more than ten times, to almost $1.7 billion. A recent survey showed that one week in March, 41 percent of American households with VCRs rented at least one videocassette. And on top of that, Americans bought 275 million blank videocassettes in 1986.

Excerpted from "Couch Potatoes: The New Nightlife," *New York Magazine*, July 20, 1987.

Check Your Comprehension

1. What are the three things that have contributed to the "Couch Potato" phenomenon?
2. What invention has contributed most to the recent trend toward staying at home, according to this article?
3. How are late marriage and childbearing related to the Couch Potato trend?
4. What does Dr. Zerubavel mean by the words "bureaucratization" and "privatization"?

Vocabulary: Antonyms and Synonyms

Think of an antonym (word that means the opposite) for each of the following vocabulary items. Then think of a synonym (word that means the same thing) for each item. The first one is done for you.

1. increase	*decrease*		*augment*
2. marriage			
3. resist			
4. relax			
5. private			
6. entertain			
7. sleep			
8. rental			
9. favorite			
10. desire			

Think About It

1. How would you answer the Gallup Poll question, "What is your favorite way of spending an evening?"

2. One of the experts quoted in this reading says that there is a trend toward working at home on computer terminals, watching movies at home on VCRs, and so on. What do you think are the advantages of this? Are there any disadvantages?

3. Have any American television programs been imported into your country? What do you think of these programs? How popular are they?

4. What are some of the negative consequences of the "Couch Potato" lifestyle that are not mentioned in this article? Make a list of at least three consequences below. Then formulate a remedy for those consequences.

CONSEQUENCE   SOLUTION

1. _____   _____

    _____   _____

2. _____   _____

    _____   _____

3. _____   _____

    _____   _____

Before You Read

Table 9.2   National Prime Time Television Schedule, 1960, 1975, and 1990

1960 Saturday Night

Network	7:30	8:00	8:30	9:00	9:30	10:00	10:30
ABC	The Roaring Twenties		Leave It to Beaver	The Lawrence Welk Show		Fight of the Week	
CBS	Perry Mason		Checkmate		Have Gun, Will Travel	Gunsmoke	
NBC	Bonanza		Tall Man	The Deputy	The Nation's Future		

1975 Monday Night

Network	8:00	8:30	9:00	9:30	10:00	10:30
ABC	Barbary Coast		NFL Monday Night Football			
CBS	Rhoda	Phyllis	All in the Family	Maude	Medical Center	
NBC	The Invisible Man		NBC Monday Night at the Movies			

1990 Tuesday Night

Network	8:00	8:30	9:00	9:30	10:00	10:30
ABC	Who's the Boss?	The Wonder Years	Roseanne	Coach	Thirtysomething	
CBS	Rescue 911		CBS Movie			
NBC	Matlock		In the Heat of the Night		Law and Order	

Ask most Americans about television and they will say it's awful. Yet, the average American watches over five hours of television every day. The author of this reading presents his theory of the "least objectionable program" as an explanation of this difference between what Americans do and what they say.

Before you read, think about the following questions:

- Have you watched American television? Do you like it?
- Do you ever feel guilty about watching too much TV?

Glossary

ratings   Measure of the number of households that watch a particular program at a particular time; such measures are important because they determine the price of television advertising.

TV Guide   Weekly magazine that contains the television schedule for each area of the country; it also contains articles about television stars and programs.

Parcheesi   Type of board game

About the Author

As he states in this article, Paul L. Klein was once an executive of the NBC network, where he was in charge of ratings.

Why You Watch What You Watch When You Watch
by Paul L. Klein

It is about time that you all stop lying to each other and face up to your problems: you love television and you view too much.

I used to be the guy in charge of the ratings at NBC, and my waking hours were filled with people either complaining about how inaccurate
5   the ratings were or, without my asking them, volunteering that they "never watch TV, because the programs stink, particularly this season."

Let's look at the facts, because only by examining the nature of the disease can we cure it, or at least make peace with it.

The truth is that you buy extra sets, color sets, and even pay a
10   monthly charge for cable television to view television. Yet when you view an evening's worth of TV you are full of complaints about what

you have viewed. But the next night you're right back there, hoping against hope for satisfying content, never really learning from experience, another night is shot. Instead of turning the set off and doing
15   something else, you persist in exercising the medium.

The fact is that you view TV regardless of its content. Because of the nature of the limited spectrum (only a few channels in each city) and the economic need of the networks to attract an audience large enough to attain advertising dollars which will cover the cost of pro-
20   duction of the TV program, pay the station carrying the program, and also make a profit, you are viewing programs which by necessity must appeal to the rich and poor, smart and stupid, tall and short, wild and tame, together. Therefore, you are in the vast majority of cases viewing something that is not to your taste. From the time you bought a set to
25   now, you have viewed thousands of programs which were not to your taste. The result is the hiding of, and lying about, all that viewing. Because of the hiding and lying, you are guilty. The guilt is expressed in the feeling that "I should have been reading instead of viewing."

It is of course much more difficult to read than to view. Reading re-
30   quires a process called *decoding*, which causes a slowdown in the information taken in by the user. TV viewing is very simple to do—kids do it better than adults because they are unencumbered by guilt—and the amount of information derived from an hour's viewing is infinitely more than is derived from an hour's reading.
35   But print has been around for a long time and it has attracted people who have learned to express themselves in this medium, so the printed content, on the whole, is superior to the TV content. Still, most of us prefer television.

Despite the lack of quality content, the visual medium is so com-
40   pelling that it attracts the vast majority of adults each day to a progression of shows that most of these people would ignore in printed form.

The process of viewing works like this:

A family has just finished dinner and one member says, "Let's see what's on TV tonight." The set gets turned on or the *TV Guide* gets
45   pulled out. If it's *TV Guide*, then the list of programs (most of which are repeats) is so unappealing that each member of the family says to himself that he remembers when *TV Guide* made an awful error in its program listings back in 1967 and maybe it has happened again.

The set is turned on whether a good program is listed or not at that
50   time. Chances are over 100 to 1 that there is nothing on that meets this or any family's taste for that moment. But the medium meets their taste.

The viewer(s) then slowly turns the channel selector, grumbling at each image he sees on the screen. Perhaps he'll go around the dial two or three times before settling on one channel whose program is *least*
55   *objectionable.*

"Well, let's watch this," someone in the family says. "There's nothing better on." So they watch. No one thinks of jogging a couple of laps around the block or getting out the old Parcheesi board. They watch whatever is least objectionable.

60   The programmers for the networks have argued that this is a "most satisfying" choice—not LOP (least objectionable program). But if it were, then why would everybody be complaining and lying about TV viewing? I don't deny that in some rare time periods, "least objectionable" is actually most satisfying, but the bulk of the time people are
65   viewing programs they don't particularly consider good, and that is why the medium is so powerful and rich.

From *TV Guide*, July 1971.

Check Your Comprehension

1. Why aren't there television programs that suit most people's individual tastes?

2. Why does the author think that people feel guilty about watching television? What is the result of this "guilt"?

3. What is Klein's theory of the "least objectionable program"?

Vocabulary: Colloquial Language

Use each of the following colloquial phrases correctly in a sentence.

1. It's about time: _____

    _____

2. It stinks: _____

    _____

3. Hoping against hope: _____

    _____

4. Another night is shot: _____

    _____

5. On the whole: _____

    _____

Think About It

1. Although the preceding article is still relevant today, it was written over twenty years ago. What clues does the article itself give you that it is old?

2. One thing that Klein mentions is the guilt people feel because they don't read more. Has television had an effect on your own reading habits? As a child, did you prefer reading or watching television?

3. The author states that there are times when nothing is on that meets a family's taste, but the "medium meets their taste." What does he mean by this? Have you ever felt this way?

4. With a partner, review the television schedule at the beginning of this section. Then, create a schedule for watching prime time television for each of those nights. If there is a conflict, you must compromise—there's only one TV set.

SATURDAY, 1960:	Time	Network	Program
	_____	_____	_____
	_____	_____	_____
	_____	_____	_____
	_____	_____	_____
	_____	_____	_____

MONDAY, 1975:	Time	Network	Program
	_____	_____	_____
	_____	_____	_____
	_____	_____	_____
	_____	_____	_____

TUESDAY, 1990:	Time	Network	Program
	_____	_____	_____
	_____	_____	_____
	_____	_____	_____
	_____	_____	_____
	_____	_____	_____

PART TWO
The Movies: The Silver Screen

Before You Read

Table 9.3   The Ten Top Money-Making Movies

1. *E.T. The Extra-Terrestrial* (1982)	$228,379,346
2. *Star Wars* (1977)	193,500,000
3. *Return of the Jedi* (1983)	168,002,414
4. *The Empire Strikes Back* (1980)	141,600,000
5. *Jaws* (1975)	129,961,081
6. *Ghostbusters* (1984)	128,264,005
7. *Raiders of the Lost Ark* (1981)	115,598,000
8. *Indiana Jones and the Temple of Doom* (1984)	109,000,000
9. *Beverly Hills Cop* (1984)	108,000,000
10. *Back to the Future* (1985)	104,237,346

Source: *Information Please Almanac,* 1989 (Boston, Mass.: Houghton Mifflin Co., 1988).

The following readings deal with two aspects of American movies—the tradition of eating popcorn, and drive-in movie theaters, which have fallen in popularity in recent years.

Before you read, think about the following questions:

* Have you ever been to a drive-in movie?

* Have you tried popcorn? What other types of snacks are popular at the movies?

Glossary

radiocarbon testing   Chemical test to determine the age of once-living things

paleobotanists   Researchers who study the ancient history of plant life

Moskowitz   Author of *Everybody's Business*, a book about business trends

sci-fi   Science fiction

About the Author

Tad Tuleja is the author of more than twenty books. He studied at Yale University and in England.

Curious Customs
by Tad Tuleja

Popcorn at the Movies

Like maple syrup and the tomato, popcorn was a gift from the New World to the Old. Radiocarbon testing has dated ears of New Mexican popping corn at 5,600 years old, and paleobotanists now generally
5 agree that popcorn was the earliest form of maize. Columbus in the West Indies and Cortes in Mexico both found the native populations utilizing popped corn as decorations, prefiguring today's popcorn "necklaces." Indians on both continents knew popcorn as food, and they used an ingenious variety of popping methods. Some tribes used hot stones
10 as popping griddles, others threw the unpopped kernels in the fire directly, and others roasted entire ears on stick spits. The pre-Incan populations of Peru even fashioned popcorn poppers out of clay.

The popping custom caught on slowly with Europeans, however, and it wasn't until the early twentieth century that popcorn became a
15 universal American snack. This was due largely to Cloid H. Smith, an Iowa farm boy who formed the American Pop Corn Company in 1914 and began selling his Jolly Time brand shortly after. Gradually, home popping became a national fad.

The introduction of popcorn into movie theaters did not happen un-
20 til a decade and a half later. According to Moskowitz and his colleagues, theater managers in the 1920s usually barred popcorn from the premises, because their patrons were distracted by the crunching. They relented only in the 1930s, after having been hounded for years by vendors selling under their marquees. Moskowitz and his colleagues sug-
25 gest that the managers changed their minds because they needed cash during the Depression and sought it from lobby concessions. This is not as plausible as it seems, for the movie industry actually thrived in those years, as the American public's need for escapist entertainment helped to fuel Hollywood's Golden Age. A more likely explanation is that with
30 the introduction of sound in the late 1920s, theatergoers were no longer distracted by the crunching and could use popcorn as they had long used chewing gum—as a means of registering, and defusing, dramatic tension.

Drive-In Movies

35   The American drive-in movie had its golden age at the same time as the drive-in restaurant, in the decade immediately following World War II, when among the leading indicators of postwar affluence were the classic gas-eaters of the 1950s and the two-car garage. But the drive-in also tied in neatly to two other sociocultural developments of that time.
40   First was the coming of age of the baby boomers. The original drive-in movie operators understood better than any sociologists that the car and its teenager cannot be parted, and in spite of advertisements aimed (often successfully) at attracting the family market, a principal source of drive-in income in those years was the carload (or carloads) of teen-
45   agers; the dominance of that market was evident in the prevalence of sci-fi and teen romance movies. Second was television. The expansion into drive-ins was a desperate move on the part of a decaying studio system to recapture some of the attention lost to the new medium, and in this effort Hollywood was mildly successful. Between 1948 and 1956,
50   the number of movie theaters in the United States was cut in half, but approximately four thousand new drive-ins helped to make up for the loss. Today many of those units have closed, but the drive-in remains an American artifact. In rural parts of the country, it retains its folkloric hold on succeeding generations of teenagers.

Excerpted from Tad Tuleja, *Curious Customs* (New York: Crown Publishers, 1987).

Check Your Comprehension

1. How did popcorn become a "universal" American snack?

2. Why was popcorn not allowed in movie theaters originally? Why does the author think that theater owners changed their minds about allowing popcorn inside?

3. What does the author mean when he says that moviegoers "could use popcorn as they had long used chewing gum—as a means of registering, and defusing, dramatic tension"?

4. What factors does the author think contributed to the popularity of the drive-in theater?

Vocabulary: Compound Words

Look at the compound words below. Divide each of them into its two parts, and then give a definition based on the definitions of the two components. The first has been done for you.

swimsuit   *swim + suit, a watersport + a set of clothing, clothing worn when participating in watersports*

1. popcorn _____ + _____ , _____

_____

2. postwar _____ + _____ , _____

_____

3. necklace _____ + _____ , _____

_____

4. gas-eaters _____ + _____ , _____

_____

5. theatergoers _____ + _____ , _____

_____

6. two-car _____ + _____ , _____

_____

7. drive-in _____ + _____ , _____

_____

8. carload _____ + _____ , _____

_____

Think About It

1. Tuleja refers to the need for "escapist entertainment." What does he mean by this? Why do you think people go to movies when times are difficult?

2. How important are movies in your own culture? How are they different (or the same) as American movies?

3. Popcorn is one of the traditional foods to eat at movies. See if you can find out other foods or beverages that are traditionally consumed during the following types of entertainment:

    a. baseball games _____

    b. movies (other than popcorn) _____

    c. picnics _____

    d. carnivals _____

    Are there any leisure activities that require special foods in your own culture?

4. The second part of this reading talks about drive-in movie theaters. There are also drive-in restaurants, drive-in grocery stores, drive-in liquor stores, and even drive-in churches! Think about the relationship between these facilities and Americans' attitudes toward cars, and then write a short essay explaining why you think Americans developed so many "drive-in" facilities.

Before You Read

Table 9.4   Academy Awards for Best Picture, 1970–1989

1970	*Patton*	1980	*Ordinary People*
1971	*The French Connection*	1981	*Chariots of Fire*
1972	*The Godfather*	1982	*Gandhi*
1973	*The Sting*	1983	*Terms of Endearment*
1974	*The Godfather, Part II*	1984	*Amadeus*
1975	*One Flew Over the Cuckoo's Nest*	1985	*Out of Africa*
1976	*Rocky*	1986	*Platoon*
1977	*Annie Hall*	1987	*The Last Emperor*
1978	*The Deerhunter*	1988	*Rainman*
1979	*Kramer vs. Kramer*	1989	*Driving Miss Daisy*

Movie critics are very important to the success or failure of a movie. In this reading, two of the most influential movie critics are discussed.

Before you read, think about the following questions:

• How do you decide which movies to see?

• What movie have you seen most recently? Did you like it?

Glossary

Chicago Sun-Times, Chicago Tribune   Competing newspapers in the city of Chicago, Illinois

PBS   Public Broadcasting Service, a noncommercial television system known primarily for its educational programs

Mutt and Jeff   Old comedy team whose comic appeal lay in the fact that each man was very different from the other

syndicated programs   Television shows that are sold independently of the national networks; therefore, they appear at different times in different cities.

Michigan rummy   Type of card game

About the Author

Richard Zoglin is a reporter for the news magazine *Time*.

"It Stinks!" "You're Crazy!"
by Richard Zoglin

Twelve years ago, Roger Ebert, film critic for the Chicago *Sun-Times* and now better known simply as "the fat one," was asked if he would appear on a new movie-review program. He was intrigued by the idea but not by the prospective costar: his archrival from the Chicago

5   *Tribune*, Gene Siskel. "The answer," Ebert recalls, "was at the tip of my tongue: no." Nor did Siskel, now frequently referred to as "the other one," relish the thought of sharing a stage with "the most hated guy in my life."

Siskel and Ebert still do not get along, at least in public, but they

10   have put that antagonism to good use. Their show, originally called *Opening Soon at a Theater Near You* and later *Sneak Previews*, went national in 1978 and soon became the highest-rated series in PBS history. In 1982 they moved to commercial syndication. Today, under the title *Siskel & Ebert & the Movies*, they reach an audience of 8 million,

15   ranking in the Top Ten of all once-a-week syndicated shows on TV.

The Mutt-and-Jeff pair are certainly the most popular and conceivably the most powerful movie critics in the country. Probably no encomium is more sought after by film publicists than "Two thumbs up—Siskel and Ebert" (reflecting their device of signaling thumbs up or

20 thumbs down for good reviews or bad). Just how much impact they have at the box office is less certain, but some in Hollywood think it is substantial. Said comedian Eddie Murphy at a recent press conference, "Siskel and Ebert go 'horrible picture,' and I'm telling you, [they] can definitely kill a movie."

25 Maybe, maybe not, but what keeps viewers tuning in is the chance to see them try to kill each other. The format of their show is simple. For each film (four are reviewed in a typical half-hour, plus an extra segment on videocassette releases) one of the pair will introduce clips, describe the plot and give a capsule review. Then comes an ad-lib pas-
30 sage in which the other offers his comments or rebuttal. The cross talk often gets testy. After the two disagreed about Susan Seidelman's comedy *Making Mr. Right*, Ebert concluded defiantly, "I enjoyed myself from beginning to end." Replied Siskel: "You usually do enjoy *yourself;* it's the *film* I didn't like." Or here is Ebert trying to convince Siskel that
35 Alan Parker's thriller *Angel Heart* is not too slow moving: "You want television . . . let's hurry and tell the story." Siskel: "Don't lay that on me . . . you know I don't watch television any more than you do." Ebert: "In that case, I'm sorry you have to be on this show."

Though bickering has made them famous, the best-kept secret
40 about Siskel and Ebert is that they agree much more than they disagree. Their tastes are generally similar (two thumbs up for *Prick Up Your Ears* and *Swimming to Cambodia;* two thumbs down for *Blind Date* and *The Secret of My Success*). Both rail regularly against teen sex comedies, violent horror films and car chases. Good movies are almost
45 always those that have "characters you can identify with."

"It is the emotional content that comes through on TV," says Ebert. "People can pick up a lot about the film through the exchange of feelings between two critics." Siskel too defends their TV-criticism against charges that it is oversimplified and superficial: "It is the distillation be-
50 tween the two of us of 39 years of writing about movies."

Is their feud a fake? "On all the movie sets I've been on," says Siskel, "I've never seen people get as angry as Roger and I get." Nor are the fights confined to the TV cameras. On a recent plane trip, Siskel was trying to teach Ebert to play Michigan rummy. At one point, Ebert ac-
55 cused Siskel of throwing a card into the wrong pile. Siskel denied it, and Ebert suddenly tossed up his seat tray. "That's it," he cried. "No more cards!" Hmmm. Conflict, characters you can identify with— definitely a thumbs up.

From *Time*, May 25, 1987.

Check Your Comprehension

1. Why didn't Siskel and Ebert want to do a television program together?
2. What does "two thumbs up" mean?
3. How seriously do Siskel and Ebert disagree about movies?
4. Read this quotation out loud, emphasizing the words written in italics:

    After the two disagreed about Susan Seidelman's comedy *Making Mr. Right,* Ebert concluded defiantly, "I enjoyed myself from beginning to end." Replied Siskel: "You usually do enjoy *yourself;* it's the *film* I didn't like."

    What does Siskel's reply mean?

Vocabulary: In Context

Rewrite the sentences below, paraphrasing the italicized word or words. You may change other words in the sentences if necessary, as long as you don't change the meaning of the sentence.

1. Film critic Roger Ebert's *archrival* is another film critic, Gene Siskel.

    _____

    _____

2. The most sought after *encomium* is "two thumbs up—Siskel and Ebert."

    _____

    _____

3. After a short summary of the film, the critics *ad-lib* and then offer a *rebuttal.*

    _____

    _____

4. *Bickering* has made Siskel and Ebert famous.

    _____

    _____

5. On each show, they show some *clips*, describe the *plots*, and give a *capsule* review.

    _____

    _____

6. Neither critic *relished* the idea of sharing the stage with the other.

    _____

    _____

Think About It

1. Millions of Americans see hundreds of movies every year. Why do you think movies are so important? What role do you think movies play in a person's life?

2. What movie have you seen most recently? Did you enjoy it? Why or why not?

3. Which movie do you think is the best you have ever seen? What made that movie so good?

4. With a partner, create your own "Siskel and Ebert" movie review show by following the steps below. (It may help to watch the Siskel and Ebert show before doing this, if that is possible.)
    a. Find two movies that both you and your partner have seen. They may be old or new movies.
    b. Each of you should select one of the movies, and write a short review of it. In your review, include information about the story, the characters, the setting, and especially whether you liked it or not.
    c. Exchange reviews, and read your partner's review. Do you agree or disagree with your partner's opinions? Make some notes about your ideas.
    d. Decide which movie you and your partner will review first. One of you will then read his or her review aloud to the class. The other will then comment on whether he or she agrees or disagrees with the review. Then the second partner will read his or her review, and the other will comment.

Synthesis

Discussion and Debate

1. Movies and television programs are among the United States' most important exports. What influence do you think these exports are having on your country?

2. On the other hand, the typical American rarely sees foreign films or television programming. What effect do you think this has on the United States?

3. Television and the movies are often blamed for society's problems. Some people believe that viewers imitate what they see in the movies. Others disagree, and say that television and movies only illustrate society's problems, they don't cause them. Which opinion do you agree with?

4. Think of another question to ask your classmates about the material covered in this chapter.

Writing Topics

1. In the United States a rating system is used to indicate who should see which films. The system is as follows:

   G: General audiences, no material that parents might find objectionable, even for very young children

   PG: Parental Guidance, there may be some material in the film that parents don't want very young children to see

   PG-13: Parental Guidance, there may be some material in the film that parents of children under the age thirteen don't want them to see

   R: Restricted, some adult material, no one under the age of seventeen admitted without an adult

   NC-17: No children under seventeen admitted

   X: No one under seventeen or eighteen admitted. This rating is generally used for "pornographic films."

   However, many people claim that the ratings system doesn't work—that it doesn't give enough information. Also, some feel that television programs should have a ratings system as well. Devise another ratings system that would give more information to people intending to see a film or watch a television program.

2. What effect do you think seeing violence in movies or on television has on young children? Write a "letter to the editor" (for publication in a newspaper) explaining to parents in your community the effect violence has on children.

3. Another issue concerning television and film is censorship. Television programs are frequently censored to remove language or scenes that the censors believe many people would object to. Movie censorship is less direct, but a certain amount of "censorship" or removal of scenes from film goes on in order to ensure that a film does not receive an X-rating.

   What do you think of censorship of television and film? Do you think it serves any purpose? Who should be responsible for censorship? Write a short essay in which you defend your ideas.

On Your Own

1. This chapter has covered only a very small portion of all the possible topics having to do with television and movies. Find another article about TV or film that interests you and read it. Give a summary of the article to the class.

2. Watch a genre of movie or television program you have never watched before. (For example, have you ever watched a soap opera, or seen a science-fiction movie?) Did you like it more or less than you thought you would?

3. In the "TV Facts" at the beginning of this chapter, it says that there is a one-in-four chance that an American has been on television. Try to find someone who has been on television (or in a movie of any type). Ask that person about his or her experience. (If you have been on television or in a film, describe to your classmates what it was like.)

4. Survey ten U.S.-born Americans about their TV and movie tastes by asking them the following questions:

   —What is your favorite current television program?
   —What is your least favorite current television program?
   —What is your favorite television program of all time?
   —What is the worst television program of all time?
   —What is the best movie you have ever seen?
   —What is the worst movie you've ever seen?

   Compare your responses with those of your classmates.

5. Look at a recent issues of a magazine that is dedicated to entertainment, for example, *Entertainment Weekly, Premiere, Cineaste, Film Quarterly, TV Guide, On Video,* and *Video Magazine.* Report to your class on the contents of the magazine.

10
Leisure:
Time to Kill

PART ONE
Sports: A Whole New Ball Game

Before You Read

Figure 10.1

```
                    K C A B L L U F
                  F Z N A B N C D E F E N S E
            B I I C X Q H O D S Z B T A C K L E
        T G U A R D P U G R C A T J I O Y Z X K K A
      R S S J J S Q O A Z I F R I E M W U D Y T R O L
    J Q X K Q O T P N R E D A E L R E E H C V U X E X P
    I E N I L D R A Y Y T F I F F B X O R U S H I N G T E C
  R H R P M R I N N S T E F R G E G X U T E A M D W K W N Y B
  G K I C K O F F D M E R E G C R H L T N N I W A O N Z A E A
  E O D N T C C X T D F B D F R E V I E C E R E D I W I L J C
  L G A F T O B T E L A A M F I E L D G O A L Z P I H N T U M
    S A L U E N M N I S C L I P P I N G O I J Q S G X V Y W
      B F P H R E K C I K E C A L P P R L K C H B H W Z A
        S V O K C A B F L A H X Q G L I N E B A C K E R
          V E S S E D I S F F O Y E S F D O Y E I S L
            V T D P W T U U E N O Z D N E R J F
              S X T S S A P L A R E T A L
                D B S C O R E T
```

WORD LIST

blitz	gridiron	referee
center	guard	rushing
cheerleader	halfback	safety
clipping	intercept	score
defense	kickoff	tackle
end zone	lateral pass	team
field goal	linebacker	time out
fifty-yard line	offsides	touchdown
first and ten	penalty	wide receiver
fullback	placekicker	win
goal posts	quarterback	wishbone

Hidden in the grid of letters (Figure 10.1) are 33 words related to football. These words are also listed in the three columns beneath the grid. (Don't worry if you don't know what they mean—only true football fans know all of these terms.) The words are hidden in the horizontal, vertical, and diagonal series of letters, but the words' letters always follow straight lines. Find and circle all 33 words. The first one, *touchdown*, is circled for you.

The author of the following reading humorously illustrates the extreme behavior of some sports fans, himself included.

Before you read, think about the following questions:

- Are you a sports fan?
- Which sport(s) do you like?

Glossary

Amtrak   National passenger railroad system of the United States

Pittsburgh Penguins   Hockey team from Pittsburgh, Pennsylvania

McNeil-Lehrer NewsHour   Daily news program broadcast by PBS

wussy   Insulting term for a nonathletic person

Jim Thorpe   Outstanding all-round athlete and famous football player who participated in collegiate, Olympic, and professional sports from approximately 1910 to 1926

Green Bay Packers, Indianapolis Colts   Football teams from Wisconsin and Indiana, respectively

lithium   Drug used to treat psychiatric disorders

Super Bowl   Final championship game of the professional football season, played at the end of January

Philadelphia Phillies   Baseball team from Philadelphia, Pennsylvania

About the Author

Dave Barry is a writer for *Tropic*, the Sunday magazine of *The Miami Herald*, a newspaper. He is also the author of the popular book *Dave Barry Turns 40*.

A Look at Sports Nuts — and We Do Mean Nuts

by Dave Barry

Today in our continuing series on How Guys Think, we explore the question: How come guys care so much about sports?

This is a tough one, because caring about sports is, let's face it, silly. I mean, suppose you have a friend who, for no apparent reason, sud-
5 denly becomes obsessed with Amtrak. He babbles about Amtrak con-
stantly, citing obscure railroad statistics from 1978; he puts Amtrak bumper stickers on his car; and when something bad happens to Amtrak, such as a train crashes and investigators find that the engineer was drinking and wearing a bunny suit, your friend becomes depressed for
10 weeks. You'd think he was crazy, right? "Bob," you'd say to him as a loving and caring friend, "you're a moron. Amtrak has NOTHING TO DO WITH YOU."

But if Bob is behaving exactly the same deranged way about, say, the Pittsburgh Penguins, it's considered normal guy behavior. He could
15 name his child "Pittsburgh Penguin Johnson" and be considered only mildly eccentric.

There is something wrong with this. And before you accuse me of being some kind of sherry-sipping ascot-wearing ballet-attending MacNeil-Lehrer-NewsHour-watching wussy, please note that I am a
20 sports guy myself, having had a legendary athletic career consisting of nearly a third of the 1965 season on the track team at Pleasantville High School ("Where the Leaders of Tomorrow are Leaving Wads of Gum on the Auditorium Seats of Today"). I competed in the long jump, because it seemed to be the only event where afterward you didn't fall down and throw up. I probably would have become an Olympic-caliber long-
25 jumper except that, through one of those "bad breaks" so common in sports, I turned out to have the raw leaping ability of a convenience store.

So, okay, I was not Jim Thorpe, but I care as much about sports as
30 the next guy. If you were to put me in the middle of a room, and in one corner was Albert Einstein, in another corner was Abraham Lincoln, in another corner was Plato, in another corner was William Shakespeare, and in another corner (this room is a pentagon) was a TV set showing a football game between teams that have no connection whatsoever with
35 my life, such as the Green Bay Packers and the Indianapolis Colts, I would ignore the greatest minds in Western thought, gravitate toward the TV, and become far more concerned about the game than I am about my child's education. And SO WOULD THE OTHER GUYS. I guarantee

it. Within minutes, Plato would be pounding Lincoln on the shoulder
40 and shouting in ancient Greek that the receiver did NOT have both feet
in bounds.

Obviously, sports connect with something deeply rooted in the
male psyche, dating back to prehistoric times, when guys survived by
hunting and fighting, and they needed many of the skills exhibited by
45 modern athletes—running, throwing, spitting, renegotiating their con-
tracts, adjusting their private parts on nationwide television, etc. So
that would explain how come guys like to PARTICIPATE in sports. But
how come they care so much about games played by OTHER guys?
Does this also date back to prehistoric times? When the hunters were
50 out hurling spears into mastodons, were there also prehistoric guys
watching from the hills, drinking prehistoric beer, eating really bad prehistoric hot dogs and shouting "We're No. 1!" but not understanding
what it meant because this was before the development of mathematics?

There must have been, because there is no other explanation for
55 such bizarre phenomena as:

—Sports-talk radio, where guys who have never sent get-well cards
to their own mothers will express heartfelt, near-suicidal anguish over
the hamstring problems of strangers.

—A guy in my office who appears to be a normal middle-age hus-
60 band and father until you realize that he spends most of his waking
hours managing a PRETEND BASEBALL TEAM. This is true. He and
some other guys have formed a league where they pay actual money to
"draft" major league players, and then they have their pretend teams
play a whole pretend season, complete with trades, legalistic memoran-
65 dums, and heated disputes over the rules. This is crazy, right? If these
guys said they were managing herds of pretend caribou, the authorities
would be squirting lithium down their throats with turkey basters,
right? And yet we all act like it's PERFECTLY NORMAL. In fact, eaves-
dropping from my office, I find myself getting involved in the discus-
70 sions. That's how pathetic I am: I'm capable of caring about a pretend
sports team that's not even my OWN pretend sports team.

So I don't know about the rest of you guys, but I'm thinking it's time
I got some perspective in my life. First thing after the Super Bowl, I'm
going to start paying more attention to things that should matter to me,
75 like my work, my friends, and above all, my family, especially my little
boy. Philadelphia Phillies Barry.

From *Tropic Magazine* (©), 1989; reprinted in *Utne Reader*, May/June, 1990.

Check Your Comprehension

1. What is the significance of the "Amtrak obsession" given as an example by the author?
2. Why does the author think that men are so interested in sports?
3. What is a simpler way of saying "sherry-sipping ascot-wearing ballet-attending MacNeil-Lehrer-NewsHour-watching wussy"?
4. Find examples of hyperbole (exaggeration) and irony in this essay. What effect do they have on you, the reader?

Vocabulary: In Context

In the table below, ten different sports are listed. Before the table, there is a list of terms associated with these sports. Write each term under the sport or sports with which it is associated.

homerun	touchdown	dribble	butterfly
hurdles	knockout	flip	puck
foul	discus	crawl	relay
jab	shortstop	quarterback	dunk
freestyle	hurdles	heavyweight	vault
slapshot	love	strike	net
backhand	spare	punt	steal

1. baseball	2. football
3. basketball	4. swimming
5. track and field	6. boxing
7. gymnastics	8. hockey
9. tennis	10. bowling

Think About It

1. What is the meaning of the phrase "sports nut"? Why do you think people become sports nuts?

2. The author talks only about men as "sports nuts." Do you know any women sports nuts? Do you think men are more likely to be sports nuts? Why?

3. If you were to become a sports nut, which sport would you follow most closely? Why are you attracted to that sport?

4. Some people like to watch sports; others like to play them. Which type are you? Explain why.

5. Research a sport that you know nothing about. If it is a game, find out the rules, and how it is played. Try to find someone who plays that sport, and ask what the sport is like, and why it is an interesting sport to participate in. Prepare a written or oral report on the new sport you have learned about.

Before You Read

Figure 10.2 A Standard Baseball Diamond

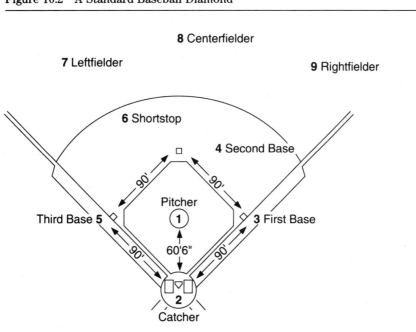

In the following reading, the author describes the activity before a baseball game. He also compares baseball with football.

Before you read, think about the following questions:

- Have you ever seen a baseball game, either in a park or on television?
- Is baseball played in your country?

Glossary

pepper   Throwing exercise in which the players throw the ball around the field quickly

batting cage   Metal frame covered with wire netting that is placed behind home plate during batting practice to keep balls from being hit into the stands where the spectators sit

dugout   Enclosure housing the bench on which the players sit when they are not in the field or batting; it is called a *dugout* because many of them are set into the ground.

clubhouse   Area in a ballpark that contains a locker room, showers, and offices; each ballpark has two clubhouses, one for the home team, and one for the visiting team.

innings   Portion of a baseball game during which each team gets a chance to score; there are nine innings in a baseball game; if at the end of nine innings, the scores of the two teams are tied (are the same), more innings are played.

baserunner   Player who, after hitting the ball, has succeeded in reaching one of the bases but has not yet returned to home plate

home plate   Spot on the field where the players bat; the base runners must cross home plate in order to score.

umpire   Official who serves as judge during the game; there are typically four umpires on the field during the game.

catcher   Player behind home plate who catches the balls the pitcher throws

pitcher   Player who stands in the middle of the diamond and throws the ball to the batter; the batter attempts to hit the ball in order to score a run—make a complete circuit of all the bases.

"Take Me Out to the Ballgame"   Most popular baseball song, often sung during ballgames by the spectators; it was written by Jack Norworth in 1908.

About the Author

Mike Whiteford is a sportswriter for the *Charleston Gazette*, a newspaper published in the city of Charleston, West Virginia.

Baseball

by Mike Whiteford

The first hints of baseball's distinction as a gentle, lighthearted affair emerge long before game time. The players are scattered about, busying themselves in conversation, autograph-signing, playing catch or pepper in front of the dugout or cards in the clubhouse. During BP—
5   batting practice for the uninitiated—the players cluster around the batting cage where laughter and extravagant smiles abound, reflecting the banter that accompanies this pre-game ritual.

By contrast, football players devote their pre-game hours to trying to arouse themselves into frenzied hostility. They pound on lockers and
10   each other. The coaches grimly review the game plan one more time. At a pre-determined moment, often specified by a television director, the players trudge from the locker room through a tunnel, ceremoniously onto the field, accompanied by the sounds of bands, cheerleaders, and a raucous crowd.

15   As game time approaches in baseball, the guys wend their way unhurriedly to their appropriate places on the bench. A more forward player might find a spot slightly to the side of the dugout, making himself more visible to the fans. A crew of relief pitchers and extra catchers shuffles off for the bullpen. At the appropriate moment the starting nine
20   jog onto the field and stir polite applause among the spectators.

At most ballparks an organist, already having played "Take Me Out to the Ball Game" and other familiar favorites, grinds out the national anthem. Then the game commences, though many of the fans are still settling into their seats or gazing around the ballpark. It's considerably
25   different, of course, at the start of a football game. All 50,000 fans are on their feet screaming. It's tradition, you understand.

Once under way, baseball offers a leisurely, relaxed pace, giving the fans, reporters, broadcasters, and players plenty of time to ponder the proceedings, exercise their imaginations, and allow their minds to
30   wander.

Baseball drama is at its best in the late innings, perhaps the eighth, with the score tied or with one team leading by a run. Base-runners

dance off first and second, trying to unnerve the pitcher, who peers
at them through the corner of his eye. The pitcher then leans toward
35   home plate, squints and stares interminably as the batter menacingly
wigwags his bat. Finally, after glancing at the runners one more time,
the pitcher delivers, the umpire bellows strike two, the entire routine is
repeated and the drama continues to build.

Except in rare instances, nothing happens at a baseball game that
40   reaches out and grabs the spectator or shouts at him; it only beckons to
him alluringly as he reflects on and considers the possibilities.

From Mike Whiteford, *How to Talk Baseball* (New York: Dembner Books, 1987).

Check Your Comprehension

1.   How would you briefly characterize the difference between pre-
     game activities in baseball and football?
2.   When is baseball most exciting?
3.   What does the author see as the advantages of baseball's slow pace?

Vocabulary: Descriptive Verbs

The 16 verbs listed below are more descriptive than the more everyday verbs that are usually used instead of them.

cluster	banter	trudge	wend
dance	shuffle	jog	gaze
ponder	wander	peer	squint
stare	bellow	beckon	reflect

1. Which of these verbs mean ways of moving?

   _____

2. Which mean ways of thinking?

   _____

3. Which mean ways of looking?

   _____

4. Which mean ways of speaking?

   _____

5. Which of these verbs mean doing certain activities slowly?

   _____

6. Which mean doing certain activities quickly?

   _____

7. Which of these verbs mean doing something loudly?

   _____

8. Which mean doing something that you do quietly?

   _____

9. Choose two of these verbs whose meanings you didn't know before and write sentences using them correctly.

   a. _____

   _____

   b. _____

   _____

Think About It

1. Do you think the author prefers baseball or football? What clues are there in this reading?

2. Sports are often said to reflect the "national character" of a country. In the United States, some would argue that football is our national game, while others say it is baseball. Which game do you think most reflects the "national character" of the United States. Why?

3. The figures below are part of the "box scores," a part of the sports pages in newspapers that tell how all the baseball teams played the day before. These box scores show the statistics of two games.

Cubs 5, Cardinals 3

ST. LOUIS	ab	r	h	bi	CHICAGO	ab	r	h	bi
MThompson rf	5	1	1	0	Walton cf	4	3	2	0
OSmith ss	4	0	0	0	Sandberg 2b	4	1	2	2
McGee cf	4	0	1	0	Grace 1b	3	0	1	2
Guerrero 1b	3	0	1	1	Dawson rf	4	0	0	0
Zeile c	3	1	0	0	DClark lf	4	0	0	0
Pendleton 3b	4	0	1	0	MiWilliams p	0	0	0	0
Hudler lf	3	1	1	1	Salazar 3b	4	1	3	0
Oquendo 2b	3	0	2	1	Dunston ss	4	0	1	1
Tewksbury p	2	0	0	0	Girardi c	3	0	0	0
Coleman ph	0	0	0	0	Bielecki p	2	0	1	0
Terry p	0	0	0	0	Assenmchr p	0	0	0	0
CWilson ph	1	0	0	0	Varsho ph	1	0	0	0
					Long p	0	0	0	0
					Wynne lf	0	0	0	0
Totals	**32**	**3**	**7**	**3**	**Totals**	**33**	**5**	**10**	**5**

St. Louis	011	000	100—3
Chicago	101	001	20x—5

Reds 1, Dodgers 0

LOS ANGELES	ab	r	h	bi	CINNINNATI	ab	r	h	bi
Sharperson 2b	4	0	0	0	Larkin ss	3	0	0	0
Gibson cf	4	0	2	0	ONeill rf	3	0	2	0
Daniels lf	4	0	1	0	Sabo 3b	3	0	0	0
Murray 1b	4	0	2	0	EDavis cf	3	0	0	0
Brooks rf	4	0	1	0	HMorris 1b	3	0	0	0
MHatcher 3b	3	0	0	0	Duncan 2b	3	0	0	0
LHarris 2b	0	0	0	0	Oliver c	3	0	0	0
Dempsey c	4	0	0	0	BHatcher lf	3	1	0	0
Crews p	0	0	0	0	Browning p	2	0	0	0
Griffin ss	4	0	2	0	Myers p	0	0	0	0
Neidlinger p	3	0	0	0					
Searage p	0	0	0	0					
Scioscia c	1	0	0	0					
Totals	**35**	**0**	**8**	**0**	**Totals**	**26**	**1**	**2**	**0**

Los Angeles	000	000	100 0
Cinninnati	000	000	01x—1

Symbols heading the columns of numbers

ab = at bat; the number of times the player had a turn trying to hit the ball

r = run; the number of times the player successfully hit the ball and ran all the way around the bases, scoring a point

h = hit; the number of times the player hit the ball

bi = batted in; the number of players that scored because the player at bat hit the ball

Symbols for the various positions

p = pitcher   *c* = catcher

ss = short stop   *1b* = first base

lf = left field   *2b* = second base

cf = center field   *3b* = third base

rf = right field

ph = pinch hitter (a batter who is sent into a game to bat in the place of another player in a pinch, as when a hit is especially needed)

The summary at the bottom of the chart shows the number of runs scored in each inning. The '×' in the last place among the numbers for the Chicago team indicates that the second part of the last inning was not played because that team had already won the game.

a. Who won the game between Los Angeles and Cincinnati?

b. Who lost the game between St. Louis and Chicago?

c. Which players were never at bat?

d. Which player was at bat the most?

e. Which player hit the most runs? What position does he play?

f. Which player got three hits? What position does he play?

g. Which players had the most "batted ins"?

h. Who were the first catchers who played in the two games?

i. How many pitchers played in the two games? Who were they?

j. In which game did both teams score in the third inning?

k. In which game and inning were three runs scored?

l. What was the total score in the fourth inning of both games?

PART TWO
Comics: Tickle Your Fancy

Before You Read

The following section has a different format from the sections found earlier in this book. You will find several comic strips or individual cartoons, drawn and written by some famous cartoonists. Answer the questions asked after each cartoon.

The New Yorker

The New Yorker is a weekly literary magazine that contains many cartoons on different subjects. The following cartoon is taken from the issue of April 24, 1989.

"Seems anybody can buy a gun these days."

1. What is happening in this cartoon?
2. What do you think the cartoon's author is commenting on?

"Doonesbury"

"Doonesbury" is a daily comic strip that appears in hundreds of newspapers across the United States. It is drawn and written by Garry Trudeau, who began the strip in the 1970s, when he was a college student. This comic strip comments extensively on current political issues, as well as contemporary American society and culture.

Explain the story told in this cartoon.

"Peanuts"

"Peanuts" is probably one of the most well-known comic strips in the world. It has been translated into many languages. Charles Schulz started the comic strip in 1950, and it is still very popular today.

What do you think of the answers the girls gave to the exam question?

"Calvin and Hobbes"

Bill Watterson began drawing Calvin and Hobbes in the 1980s. It depicts a mischievous boy and his toy tiger. "Calvin and Hobbes" has become one of the most popular comic strips in the United States.

1. How would you describe Calvin?
2. How does Calvin's reply to Hobbes relate to what you know about American television viewing habits?

"Garfield"

Garfield is a fat, lazy yellow cat and the famous star of a comic strip drawn and written by Jim Davis. In his comic strip home, he lives with his owner Jon and a dog, Odie. Garfield has been "merchandised" widely: that is, you can buy Garfield dishes, towels, clothing—just about anything you want.

1. Why are the mice bringing Garfield a piece of pie?
2. What do the mice mean by a "real" cat?

Brian Orr

Brian Orr is a cartoonist who lives in Colorado. He drew this cartoon especially for this book.

1. What is the woman in the foreground doing? Why?
2. Do you find this cartoon funny? Why?

Synthesis

Discussion and Debate

1. Many people consider sports or comics a "waste of time and money." What do you think? What purpose do either sports or comics serve?
2. Both sports teams and the producers of comic strip characters participate in "merchandising" themselves or their creations—the selling of products that have team names or pictures of the comic strip characters on them (for example, Mickey Mouse watches, baseball team t-shirts). Have you ever purchased any of this type of merchandise? Why or why not?
3. How do you like to "waste time"?
4. Think of another question to ask your classmates about the ideas in this chapter.

Writing Topics

1. Write one or two paragraphs describing a favorite leisure time activity of your own country that isn't practiced in the United States.
2. Write a letter to a friend back home describing how you spent your last "free" day—a day during which you didn't work or study, but did the things you wanted to do. (If you haven't had such a day, think of how you would like to spend a free day.)
3. Write a short essay describing the similarities and differences between how people spend their leisure time in your country and in the United States.

On Your Own

1. Read other comic strips besides the ones presented in this chapter. Which ones do you like? Which ones don't you like?
2. Find a story in the sports pages that interests you and read it. Summarize the story for your classmates.
3. Political cartoons often appear on the editorial pages of the newspaper, and deal with issues relevant to the day's events. Look at some political cartoons in a recent newspaper. Bring one or two to class to discuss with your classmates.

4. The following films deal with sports. Rent one of them from your local video tape store if you can and watch it.

   Semi-Tough (football)   *Field of Dreams* (baseball)
   Brian's Song (football)   *Bad News Bears* (baseball)
   Chariots of Fire (running)   *Bull Durham* (baseball)
   North Dallas Forty (football) *Pumping Iron* (weightlifting)

5. Survey ten U.S.-born Americans about their leisure time. Ask them the following questions:

   —Do you participate in any sports? Which ones?
   —Do you watch any sports? Which ones?
   —Which comic strip is your favorite?
   —Which comic strip is your least favorite?
   —How many hours a week do you spend in leisure activities?

   Summarize your results and compare them with those of your classmates.

Index

TEXT CREDITS

PHOTO CREDITS